THE RESTAURANT COMPENDIUM FOR THE CURIOUS

THE RESTAURANT COMPENDIUM FOR THE CURIOUS

Trivia, lists, bests, worsts, facts, opinions, history, wit, wisdom, sayings, humor, inside looks, deep dives, trends, and other essential information

JOHN T. SELF, PHD
Restaurant manager, restaurant owner, restaurant aficionado

Copyright © 2022 by John T. Self

All rights reserved

This book or any portion thereof may not be reproduced or used in any manner whatsoever without the express written permission of the publisher except for the use of brief quotations in a book review.

ISBN 978-0-578-82671-4

Other Books by John Self

The New Restaurant Manager (2021)

The New Restaurant Manager Part 2 (2022)

The Promotable Manager (2022)

To Deb
Thank you for being the drive and inspiration to accomplish anything

Every effort has been made to ensure that the information contained within *The Restaurant Compendium for the Curious* is accurate and up to date. The author would be pleased to be notified of errors or omissions that would improve future editions.

Please send all comments or suggestions to the author at servicedoc@yahoo.com

CONTENTS

Chapter I: Trivia, Small Stuff, Trifles, Minutia, Unimportant,
  Incidentals, Details, Trivialities, Frippery, and Small Potatoes .. 11
   Trivia 13
   Origins and Beginnings 41
   Restaurant Event Timeline 50
   US Trends Over the Decades 62
   Holidays Celebrating Restaurants, Foods, and Drinks 67

Chapter II: Funny Stuff 71
   Jokes 73
   Groaners 75
   Double Groaners 76
   Shifts from Hell 79
   Annoying! 83

Chapter III: The World's Most Unusual, Odd, Quirky, Weird Restaurants
   and Why We Love Them 87

Chapter IV: Highly Opinionated 97
   Books, TV, Movies, Music, and Media, Oh My! 99
   Let's Eat! 114
   I'll Drink to That! 147
   The World's Best Restaurant Quotes, Names,
      and Other Words 179
   People, People, People 195

Chapter V: Inside Restaurants 213
   The Chains 216
   It's All About the Money 241
   Bad Stuff 248
   The Business of Restaurants 262
   Significant Impacts and Massive Changes 265

Chapter I

TRIVIA AND THE SMALL STUFF

Trifles, minutia, unimportant, incidentals, details, trivialities, frippery, and small potatoes

TRIVIA

The year that sliced bread invented
("the greatest invention since sliced bread…")?
1928

Which US capital city is the only one with no McDonald's?
Montpelier, Vermont

P. F. Chang's
(**P**aul **F**leming and Philip **Chiang**
(Chiang was simplified to Chang)

Arby's
Got its name from its founders, brothers Forrest and Leroy Raffel.
(**R**affel **B**rothers. RB's, get it?)

F.O.O.
Initials you want by your reservation: Friend Of the Owner

What is the *only* correct response when a chef gives an order?
"Yes, chef!"

Red or Green?
The official state question of New Mexico.
Really.
This refers to the color of chili sauce.
If you order 'Christmas', you'll get both

Probably bigger than yours.
The world's largest wine collection
Milestii Mici, Moldova
The cellar holds around 2 million bottles of wine

Why Carl's Jr. is Carl's Jr when there is no Carl, Jr

Nope, Carl Karcher did not have a son named Carl Karcher, Jr.. His original restaurant was 'Carl's Drive-In Barbecue Restaurant' which grew to five locations with hamburgers as its biggest seller. He decided to open a separate and smaller burger place, called 'Carl's Jr'.

How many ounces are in a keg of beer?
1984

Daquiri, Cuba
is where US troops first landed in Cuba during the Spanish American War in 1898.

Wine cork enthusiasts are called
helixophiles

McDonald's
is the 7th largest real estate company in the world with over $41 billion in real estate (estimated)

Commas Save Lives 2
No comma: We're eating grandma (Bad)
Comma: We're eating, grandma (Good)

What is the practice of eating horse meat called?
Hippophagy

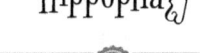

Whataburger
The founder loved flying which is why the logo looks like wings in flight

There are over 1,000,000 restaurants in the US

Michigan
is the only state that protects overweight people from discrimination when it passed this 1977 law.

Major General George Owen Squier

(West Point graduate and PhD from Johns Hopkins University) started Musak. He liked the company name Kodak, so he took the first three letters from the word "music," added the letters "ak" from Kodak, and Muzak was born

---

1936

40-hour workweek begins. Overtime begins in the US

During the great depression of the 1930s many Americans were unemployed. To get employers to hire more, employers had to pay 50% more per hour if worked over 40 hours per week.

The first Chick-fil-A

opened as The Dwarf Grill
in Atlanta, Georgia.

McDonalds has a vegetarian-only restaurant.
It opened in 2012 in

India.

About 10% of Americans

eat Thanksgiving dinner in a restaurant

The points or teeth of the fork are called

'tines'

Trivia and the Small Stuff

At one point, Clifton's Cafeteria, in Los Angeles, was the largest public cafeteria in the world. It opened in 1931 and closed in 2018.

According to Guinness World Records,
the world's highest restaurant is the
Heavenly Jin Restaurant,
inside the J Hotel Shanghai Tower, in Shanghai, China.
It is 1,825 feet above ground. The J Hotel is on the top floors
of the Shanghai Tower, the tallest building in China,
and the third tallest in the world.

Trader Vic's original name was
Hinky Dinks

Chicago food trucks must stay 200 feet away from brick-and-mortar restaurants and must be equipped with a GPS so "proximity bans" can be enforced.

The Margherita pizza was named after
Margherita of Savoy,
Queen consort of Italy from 1878 to 1900.

Yes, a street food vendor has a Michelin Star!
Singapore's Chan Hon Meng, has two kiosks:
"Hill Street Tai Hwa Pork Noodle" and
"Hong Kong Soya Sauce Chicken Rice and Noodle"
World's first street food vendor to win a Michelin Star

Blood Alcohol Concentration (BAC)
limit is 0.08 for drivers over 21 in the United States.
A BAC of 0.08 means you have eight units of alcohol for every 10,000 units of blood.

Commas save lives
With comma: Let's eat, grandma (good)
Without comma: Let's eat grandma (bad)

Most expensive Big Mac:
Switzerland
Least expensive Big Mac:
Russia

By 1926, the types of silverware had gotten out of hand.
For example, there were 15 different forks for special occasions.
In response, Secretary of Commerce Herbert Hoover
and the Sterling Silverware Manufacturers limited the number of
separate pieces in any silverware pattern to 55.

'Fish and chips'
was one of the few foods in the UK not subject to rationing during
WW I and WW II

Mai tai
means "good" in Tahitian

A butt is a real unit of measurement for a cask of wine.
A buttload is about 130 gallons

US city with most restaurants per capita
San Francisco
Over 39 per 10,000 households

Today, we want people to smile for the camera,
so we get them to say "cheese."
In the early 19th century, they wanted more of a stern and proper
look, so they said "prunes."
Try it. It definitely works.

Savannah celebrates New Year's Eve by dropping a big red to-go cup;
not a boring ball like New York City

Beethoven
had his coffee made with exactly 60 beans per cup.

Urinals are called *pissoirs* in France

Americans drink alcohol the most between the months of
December and March.
Fourteen of the year's biggest drinking days (on which users have an
average BAC above 0.08%) happen in this time period.

The Restaurant Compendium for the Curious

US city with lowest percentage of chain restaurants is
San Francisco
with 7%.

US city with highest percentage of chain restaurants
Independence, Missouri
with 60.6%

Largest restaurant chain by number
McDonald's and Subway
McDonald's +- 39,000 Subway +- 37,000 restaurants
Largest restaurant chains by $
Starbucks and McDonalds
Starbucks $24 billion, McDonald's +$19 billion

A Rum Ration
was given to British sailors until 1970, but ended in the US in 1862

In 1825, a judge named Jean Anthelme Brillat-Savarin published *The Physiology of Taste: Or Mediations on Transcendental Gastronomy*, in which he stated that the ideal room temperature for a dinner party was 60 to 68 degrees F

Don the Beachcomber was originally Don's Beachcomber. The owner and founder, Ernest Raymond Gantt, later changed his name to Donn Beach

Route 66's oldest restaurant still in operation is the Ariston Café in Litchfield, Illinois. It opened on Route 66 in 1935

Trivia and the Small Stuff

Grog

Grog is a word that means alcohol. It originally came from the word 'grogram', which is a type of fabric. Admiral Edward Vernon, of the British Navy, was known as "Old Grog" because he wore a cloak of grogram. But, in 1740, he issued the very unpopular, very hated, not liked "Order to Captains No. 349," which watered down the rum ration. From then on, navy rum became known as grog and not in a nice way.

The plot of the Pixar film *Ratatouille* has its roots in French Chef Bernard Loiseau's life story. Chef Loiseau committed suicide in 2003 when it was speculated that he was going to lose a Michelin star and be downgraded from 3 to 2 Michelin stars.

$366.12

First day sales for Ray Kroc's first McDonald's

Denny's Grand Slam

began in Atlanta in honor of Hank Aaron

The typical US urinal uses 1 gallon of water per flush, is flushed 20 times per day, and uses 7,300 US gallons of water per year

McDonald's is called "Jingongmen" in China
Roughly meaning
"Golden Arches"

Why liquors are called "spirits"
The word 'alcohol' probably came from the Arabic word 'al-ghawl', which literally means spirit and is mentioned in the Koran as a spirit or demon that intoxicates

---

Harland Sanders says his
"Original Recipe"
of 11 herbs and spices includes salt and pepper and that the rest "stand on everybody's shelf."

There is no difference between ghost kitchens, cloud kitchens, dark kitchens, and virtual kitchens. They all sell made-to-order food or meals by online orders for delivery only.

The original
Five Guys Burgers
were the 4 sons and the father, but, after one more son was born, the 5 sons are the five guys

---

There are no more officer clubs in the US military. In 1970 there were around 100 but began to decline in the 90's because of perceived alcoholism, inequality, and competition from civilian restaurants

---

Eating utensils are made of silver because it reacts the least with food and is the reason that
"Silverware"
came to be. The invention of silver-plating caused silverware to go

from only for the wealthy to everyone else

Chop Suey
may have come from the Cantonese dish "tsap seui," meaning miscellaneous leftovers

Houston, Texas
has the most McDonald's, the most Burger Kings, the most Subways, and the most Taco Bells of any other city. But it's only 5th in Starbucks

The Happy Meal
started in 1978

"Foodie"
became a thing in 1982

Not the best cocktail party ice breaker:
Caprophagous – Excrement Eating

Bistro
– got its name when Russian soldiers occupied Paris in 1815. When ordering food, they would yell out "Bistro, Bistro." *Bystro* means hurry in Russian

There are no franchises in Starbucks in the US or Canada*
*But you *can* become a licensee in the US and Canada
However, you *can* get a Starbucks franchise
outside of the US and Canada

Women make up two out of three of all tipped employees
(hair stylists, manicurists, etc). Food servers and bartenders are
roughly half of all tipped employees and 70% of those are women.

Haus Hiltl
is the oldest vegetarian restaurant in the world.
Founded in 1898 in Zurich, Germany and is still going.

Pizza toppings
Most popular - Pepperoni
Least popular - Anchovies

MacDonald's is the world's largest
toy distributor
because of the Happy Meal.

First McDonald's in Beijing, China opened in 1991.
At the time, it was the world's largest McDonald's, with
28,000 square feet, seating for 700, with 1,000 employees.
It closed in 1996 to make way for a shopping center

World's most expensive cocktail:
27,321 dirhams equals $7,438.33 US Dollars
Burj Al Arab Hotel, Dubai, United Arab Emirates

All bourbon is whiskey, but not all whiskey is bourbon
All cognac is brandy, but not all brandy is cognac
All mezcal is tequila, but not all tequila is mezcal

You *did* know that Wendy's was named for founder Dave Thomas' daughter. But did you know that Wendy was a nickname?

Her real name is Melinda Lou

The Finns love their saunas!

Burger King has a sauna in its restaurant in Helsinki, Finland

The sauna can accommodate 15 people for groups, birthday parties, or other celebrations. The spa also has a washroom, dressing room, toilet, and TV

Difference between a banquette and a booth

Booths: Two benches facing each other meant to create a cozy, private seating experience. Can be in a U shape.
Banquette: Usually an upholstered fixed bench seat, sometimes placed along a wall, with chairs on the other side. Think of a banquette as half of a booth; two banquettes facing each other would create a booth.

The Japanese Fugu

(a kind of pufferfish) contains tetrodotoxin which is up to 1,200 times more poisonous than cyanide and has no known antidote.

There are no Red Lobsters in Massachusetts and Maine

According to the FBI, at least 10,490 violent crimes were committed in U.S. restaurants in 2020, making the industry the eighth-most likely place for Americans to be attacked (about 2% of all attacks).

1806
The US Navy switched from rum (grog) to Rye whiskey

Most expensive restaurant stock price
Chipotle (CMG)

The Origin of the word "booze"

The first reference to the word "booze," meaning "alcoholic drink," appear in the English language around the 14th century as "bouse." The modern spelling appeared in the 17th century. The word "booze" might come from the Dutch word "búsen," which meant "to drink excessively" or "to get drunk."

Urinal
The invention of the urinal in 1866 was a big deal for restaurants because more urinals could be placed in a men's restroom than sit-down toilet stalls and users spend less time using a urinal than a conventional sit-down toilet.

In 1990, the first McDonald's Restaurant opened in the Soviet Union and served more than 50,000 customers per day

Trivia and the Small Stuff

In Russia, the Big Mac is called
the Bolshoi Mak
(Bolshoi means big in Russian)

The many hash browns of Waffle House

Smothered – with sauteed onions
Covered – melted American cheese added
Chunked – chunks of grilled hickory smoked ham added
Diced – grilled tomatoes added
Peppered – jalapeño peppers added
Capped – with grilled button mushrooms
Topped – with Bert's Chili (chili beans, Jimmy Dean sausage, tomato, and onion)
Country – sausage gravy added

World's largest wine cellar
Milestii Mici, Moldova

There are around 34 miles of tunnels in this wine cellar, so you'll need
a car or bike to get around. You can take a one-day guided tour
which includes a wine tasting. The cellar is made of limestone
that keeps the temperature between 54- and 57-degrees F all year.

Why say cream and sugar and not sugar and cream?

Because it is easier to say. But here's the technical reason. Anytime a related pair of items are treated as one, like cream and sugar or name and address, the single syllable word goes first with "and" in the middle, and the multisyllable word last. Exception: bacon and eggs.

The many words for beer

Angel's food, dragon's milk, go-by-the-wall, lift leg, mad dog, stride wide, cold one, whoresonne, nectar of the gods, ale, brew, lager, malt, barley pop, bitter, cold-one, brewage, brewski, home brew, belt, nip, peg, barley-bree/barley-broo, guest beer, amber brew, shandy, session beer, slops, yard, kvass, porter, stout, swanky, pint, quaff, suds, sauce, tipple, firewater, John Barleycorn, Dutch courage, snort, tot

Jack in the Box in Zulu:

Udoli ohlala ebokisini ukuthi ufuna ukusabisa abantu abaningi

Nearly one-third of all deaths of 15- to 20-year-olds are the result of a motor vehicle crash and about 35 percent of those fatalities are alcohol-related, according to the National Highway Traffic Safety Administration.

In the US, the maximum blood alcohol content (BAC) levels are all .08, but punishments vary widely. Arizona, Tennessee, and Georgia have mandatory jail time for first offenders, while in Wisconsin, a first-offense drunk driving offense isn't a crime. It's a civil infraction that results in a ticket. Even though a first offense DUI is not a criminal violation, it stays on your traffic record for life. Another offense within ten years *is* a criminal second offense, and a third offense at any time in your life is a third criminal offense

Ray Kroc bought the McDonald brothers out in 1961 for $2.7 million.

Trivia and the Small Stuff

Deipnophobia –
the fear of dinner party conversations

If you have a pizza with a radius Z and thickness A,
its volume would be Pi*Z*Z*A

Brits eat 97% of the world's
baked beans

White Castle burgers invented
the hamburger bun

The Las Vegas Strip is not actually in Las Vegas.
It is actually in Paradise
(which includes McCarran International Airport and UNLV).

Syllabubs (not to be confused with syllabus)
An American drink from the colonial period made of cream, Rhenish wine, sugar, and lemons or alternatively, heavy whipping cream, sherry, lemon, sugar, and red wine.

Which is right? I'm so confused!
Many hands make light work

Too many cooks spoil the broth

How the Restaurant got its name
The word restaurant comes from the French verb 'restaurer' meaning "to restore oneself." Before 1789, the first true French restaurants were health-food shops selling only bouillon.

Why do we use salt and pepper to flavor our food?
Might be because the King of France, Louis XIV, demanded that his food be seasoned only with salt and pepper.

The world's largest Burger
In 2017, Mallie's Sports Grill & Bar in Detroit, Michigan produced the world's largest commercially sold burger when they made a 1,794-pound cheeseburger that is actually on the menu. (Just give them 3 days' notice). The burger is topped with 300 pounds of cheese, tomatoes, onions, pickles, and lettuce. The bun alone, donated by the Michigan Bread Company, weighed 250 pounds.
When it was finally constructed, the burger measured three feet tall and five feet wide.

Today Mallie's Sports Grill and Bar's menu (Southgate, Michigan) has a 10-pound burger ($75), and of course, the 1,800-pound burger, which costs a reasonable $10,000. And, if you're still hungry, they also offer a 2-pound taco.

Why is splitting the bill called "going Dutch" or "Dutch treat"?
Today, Dutch treat means that each person pays their own way. But during the English - Dutch trade wars (mid-1600's to late 1700's), the two countries were not the best of friends and "going Dutch" became an insult.

How did saloons with swinging doors lock up after closing?

Ronald M. James wrote in his book "Virginia City: Secrets of a Western Past," that most saloons didn't have swinging doors. That's because it was just too cold in winter and too windy in summer to be practical. But some saloons did, but the doors were on the inside; the outside doors were normal, solid doors on the saloon entrance. When opened, they laid flat against each side of the building but could be shut (and padlocked) during bad weather or when the saloon closed.

Watch your Ps and Qs

Means Pints and Quarts. A customer would say to a bartender so the bartender would give the correct amount.

Ok, so you know Saturday is the busiest day to eat out and probably know that Friday is the second busiest day, but what is the *third* busiest day to eat out?

Sunday

Tequila

takes its name from the city of Tequila, in the Mexican state of Jalisco, the main production area for tequila.

The first food eaten in space was

apple sauce

Most popular ethnic foods in the US
Italian
Mexican
Chinese

Most expensive burger in the US?
$777
Le Burger Brasserie at Paris Las Vegas Hotel and Casino, Las Vegas, Nevada

Most expensive meal in the United States
Masa, New York

The correct spelling of the word that means proprietor or owner of a restaurant:
Restaurateur (no n)

At its peak in 1960, Howard Johnson had 607 independently owned restaurants making it the largest restaurant chain in the United States. Today, there is only one, in Lake George, New York.

7-Up
was originally known as Lithiated Lemon

Sweet Breads
Sweet bread is kind of like Greenland. It's not sweet, just like Greenland is not green. Sweetbreads are not sweet, and they're not even bread. Sweetbread is made of the thymus gland of a calf or lamb

White Castle meat patties are square shaped with five holes in them
so they can be cooked without having to be turned over

Myth? It is illegal for a restaurant to refuse cash payment.

Not completely true. There is no *federal* law that prohibits
businesses from going cashless, but there are some states
that require businesses to accept cash.

McDonald's Big Mac is called Maharaja Mac in India
and is made of mutton

Why are burgers and fries served together?

Since burgers are finger food, the side needed to be a finger food too
so French fries fit perfectly. A big plus for fries is that every
condiment that goes on a burger (ketchup, mayo, mustard)
go perfectly on fries too

Pat O'Brien's was originally 'Mr. O'Brien's Club Tipperary'

Papa Murphy's started as a merger
with Papa Aldo's Pizza and Murphy's Pizza in 1995

Why liquors are called "spirits"

The word *alcohol is* thought to have come from either of two
old Arabic words. Either *al-ghawl*, which literally means
spirit and is mentioned in the Qur'an as a spirit or demon

that gives wine its intoxicating effects

Bern's Steakhouse in Tampa, Florida has over 6,500 labels and 500,000 bottles in its wine collection

---

$2.7 Million
Average annual sales of a McDonald's

Pizza Hut
delivered the first pizza to the International Space Station (ISS) in 2001. It was delivered by a Russian rocket and the Russian Space Agency and cost Pizza Hut about 1 million dollars for the delivery

---

Most popular day to eat out is Saturday
Slowest is Monday

Margarita
means 'daisy' in Spanish

Myth: Absinthe is hallucinogenic and is banned in the US.
Truth: No, it is not. Twice

Myth: "Tip" stands for "To Insure Promptness."
Truth: Nope. It's a myth. Well, no one really knows

Myth: Restaurateur is spelled with an n and pronounced with an n

Truth: Spell – Restaurateur. No n! *Not* restauranteur.
Pronounce – Since there is no n, don't pronounce the missing n.

Welsh Rarebit

Hot cheese sauce served over toast, then grilled or toasted. This is not just "cheese on toast," oh no. The cheese sauce includes butter, milk, beer, hot sauce, dry mustard, ground black pepper, flour, salt, and Cheddar cheese, and often egg yolks or heavy cream

Difference between shrimp and prawns

Most shrimp live in saltwater. Most prawns live in fresh water. Shrimp are generally smaller than prawns, but for cooking, the taste, texture, and nutrition are the same.

Myth – Diamond Jim Brady

ate enormous quantities of food in the early 1900's. One restaurant owner called him "the best 25 customers I have." He was reported to have eaten for breakfast a gallon of orange juice, hominy, eggs, corn bread, muffins, flapjacks, chops, fried potatoes, and a steak. At lunch, 2 or 3 dozen clams and oysters, 2 or 3 deviled crabs, broiled lobsters, a joint of beef, salad, and several pies. Dinner started with 2 or 3 dozen oysters, half a dozen crabs, two bowls of soup, six lobsters, two whole ducks, a sirloin steak, vegies, and dessert, a 12 egg souffle, finishing with a box of chocolates
Truth: It's possible that Diamond Jim may have eaten like that occasionally, but only occasionally

Difference between supper and dinner?

Many of us think of supper and dinner as the same, but dinner refers to the largest meal of the day, whether it be morning, noon, or evening. Supper, however, *almost* always refers to a lighter evening meal.

Here's the almost. Since supper had its roots in farming, the large meal of the day would be eaten at noon since there was still a lot of work to do. This was followed by a lighter meal in the evening.

When people migrated to the cities and suburbs, they were still at work at noon, which meant that the big meal moved to the evening meal *after* work.

What happens when a fly lands on your food?

Houseflies have no teeth, so when a housefly lands on your food, it puts saliva on the food to make it into a liquid, so they can suck it through their nose. Basically, they keep spitting and throwing up until the food is liquid. Reminds me of one of my uncles.

I know. Nice.

But what's worse is they eat pretty much anything, from garbage and rotting meat, to feces. But, for most healthy adults, food doesn't need to be thrown out if a fly just lands on it and immediately takes off, because the fly has not had enough time to spit and throw up. Very comforting.

Difference between Cappuccino & Latte

A traditional cappuccino has equal amounts of espresso, steamed milk, and foamed milk. A latte has more steamed milk with very little foam on top. Another difference is that in a cappuccino, you can see the layers, while in a latte the espresso and steamed milk are mixed.

The Italian word latte means milk. This could cause you to get milk if you just say latte. Try saying 'caffe latte.'

2,500 years ago in China, knives were the common eating utensil. Confucius helped chopsticks gain popularity. A vegetarian, he believed that knives at the dinner table would not bring calm to meals.

Because of its resemblance, the word for the modern fork came from the devil's pitchfork

A "cadena"

is a specialty box meant to hold your personal knife and fork when you were invited to dinner parties in the 14th century

Difference between tequila and mezcal?

They are both made from the agave cactus. Mezcal can be made from many types of the agave plant, but tequila must be made from only the blue agave cactus

Tequila agave is steamed in ovens while Mezcal agave is cooked in underground pits, producing the distinctive mezcal smoky flavor
Mezcal must be made in one of nine Mexican states: Durango, Guerrero, Guanajuato, Michoacán, Oaxaca, Puebla, San Luis Potosí, Tamaulipas, and Zacatecas

Mezcal's alcohol content (55%) is higher than tequilas (40%)

- Blanco is unaged tequila.
- Reposado is tequila aged 2 to 12 months in oak barrels.
- Añejo tequila is aged 1 to 4 years in oak, commonly used for drinking straight, not for mixing in cocktails.

Busiest Restaurant Holidays
Mother's Day
(10% Breakfast, 25% brunch, 45% lunch, 47% dinner)
Valentine's Day
Father's Day

Cordon Bleu
French for blue ribbon

Veuve Clicquot Champagne
means "the Widow Clicquot"
Nicole-Barbe Clicquot's husband died in 1796 and she carried on with the wine business after his death

AGE is Just a Number

17
Fred DeLuca founded Subway to help pay college tuition

18
Antoine Alciatore opened Antoine's Restaurant in New Orleans

19
Bill Darden opens his first restaurant, The Green Frog. Later he would develop The Red Lobster chain and, oh yeah, a giant company named after him, Darden Restaurants Incorporated (DRI)

24
Paul Liebrandt becomes the youngest chef to receive a 3-star rating from the New York Times. 2011 Documentary on him called "A Matter of Taste"

26
Evan Goldstein, a San Francisco sommelier, becomes the youngest person ever to pass the Master Sommelier exam in England in 1987

32
Lynsi Snyder becomes the youngest female billionaire in the US. She is the daughter of Harry and Esther Snyder, founders of In-N-Out Burger

33
Howard Schultz buys Starbucks, a Seattle coffee bean business and begins to open coffee shops

33
Norman Brinker opens Brinks Coffee shop, his first restaurant. He went on to found Steak and Ale and later, bought Chili's restaurant which became Brinker International (Chili's, Maggiano's, It's Just Wings)

The Restaurant Compendium for the Curious

50
Julia Child wrote her first cookbook

56
Ray Kroc opens his first McDonald's

65
George Church Sr. founded Church's Chicken in San Antonio, Texas in 1952

65
Colonel Sanders (Harland Sanders) opens the first Colonel Sanders' Kentucky Fried Chicken

65
Dave Thomas, Wendy's founder, goes back to school to finally earn his degree

Origins and Beginnings

Alka-Seltzer - 1931 a combination of sodium bicarbonate, aspirin, and anhydrous citric acid, used for the relief of heartburn, acid indigestion, and stomach aches.

Automatic espresso machine – 1946. Patented by Italian inventor, Achille Gaggia.

Bloody Mary (vodka, tomato juice, salt and pepper, Tabasco sauce, Worcestershire sauce, lemon juice) invented in 1921 at Harry's Bar in Paris.

Bock beer -AD 1200 – invented in Einbeck, Germany. Bock is German for male goat.

Bottled Beer – 1869- introduced by Francis Manning-Needham, an English brewer will be used by most major brewers because they are hygienic and reusable.

Caesar salad – Created by Italian born, Mexican chef Caesar Cardini around 1924.

Cash Register: 1878. James J. Ritty (US). He owned a restaurant in Dayton, Ohio and felt he was getting ripped off when customers paid. He invented the "Incorruptible Cashier," the world's first cash register.

Chateaubriand Steak was actually invented by Francois Rene de Chateaubriand's chef. A thick cut of tenderloin, usually big enough for two, broiled and served with potatoes, sauteed mushrooms, vegies, and bearnaise sauce. Chateaubriand served in the French military, was an influential writer, explored the American Wilderness, and was French ambassador to Sweden, Prussia, the United Kingdom, and the Papal States.

Chicken wings (also called Buffalo wings)– Created in Buffalo, New York at the Anchor Bar in 1964. Usually served coated in hot sauce with celery sticks and bleu cheese sauce. Restaurants and bars absolutely loved wings because beer sales always jumped when customers ate wings and customers loved them because they could be easily shared.

Clean Plates – By 1655 French society used a clean plate for each new food dish, while the English continued to dine off trenchers (wooden platters).

Cocktail – One version is that it was invented in 1776 by a barmaid, Betsy Flanagan. She had decorated the bar with tail feathers from poultry at an Elmsford, New York tavern when serving a customer, a mixed drink with a feather. A customer saw it and wanted one. Another version is that the cocktail got its name in 1795 from the French word, coquetier, or egg cup, that was used by New Orleans' Antoine Amade Peychaud to make the first mixed drinks called cocktails.

Coffee – Coffee first appeared in London from Turkey and sold for 5 British pounds per *ounce* ($1,312 in 2021 dollars)

Continental breakfast –The American continental breakfast is copied from the light morning meals found in mainland Europe ("the continent"), usually consisting of pastries, bread, jam, fruit, and coffee. American hotels loved the continental breakfast, since all the foods can be self-serve requiring few staff and can be left out for a relatively long period of time.

Credit Card - The history of credit cards as we know them today began in 1950, when Diners Club launched the first modern credit card. Credit card history also includes a number of important milestones from 1950 to today, including the introduction of magnetic stripe verification in the 1960s and EMV chip technology in 2010. The term credit card was first used in Edward Bellamy's novel "Looking Backward" in 1887.

Daiquiri – (rum, lime juice, and sugar) Daiquiri gets its name from the city of Daiquiri, Cuba around 1900.

Egg McMuffin – Originally based on an egg benedict. The very first Egg McMuffin was sold at the Belleville, New Jersey location in 1972 but took till 1975 to make it to all McDonalds.

Fajitas - In the 1930s, ranch hands were often partly paid by being given lesser cuts of beef, called skirt steak. These were cut into strips, cooked over coals, then into tortillas. The word faja is Spanish for "strip," or "belt, so fajitas are small strips or belts. In 1969 Houston, María Ninfa Rodríguez Laurenzo (Mama Ninfa) was from the area of Mexico where fajitas were used. She added chairs and tables to the front room of her tortilleria and started selling tacos with the fajitas.

Fish and chips – By 1864, steam trawlers could keep fish fresh by packing them in ice. Restaurants would deep fry and serve them in newspapers with deep fried potatoes, sprinkled with vinegar.

French Fries – Known as "chips" in the United Kingdom and "pomme frites" in France. Americans first ate fries during World War I when they were stationed in Belgium. These should have been called Belgian fries, because the Belgians spoke French, but since they heard French being spoken, the Americans mistakenly called them French fries.

Historians claim potatoes were fried in Belgium as early as the late 1600s when poor villagers would often eat small fried fish they caught in the river. But in the winter, the villagers switched to eating potatoes, slicing, and frying them just like they did the fish.

Gas oven – 1838. The Reform Club in London installed first gas oven to replace coal or wood.

Gimlet (gin, fresh lime juice and sugar), was created by Sir T.O. Gimlette, a British naval surgeon to get sailors to have some form of citrus to prevent scurvy, a disease caused by the lack of vitamin C.

Grand Marnier. Marnier was the first name of Marnier Lapostolle who created the liqueur Marnier. The name Grand Marnier came about when Cesar Ritz playfully named it Grand Marnier because Marnier Lapostolle was quite short.

Hamburger – Probably originated in Russia in the Middle Ages when the Tartars would eat raw meat that was scraped and shredded then mixed with salt, pepper, and onion juice. German sailors brought the recipe back home to Hamburg, Germany. Instead of eating it raw, they broiled the outside. German immigrants then brought the hamburg steak to the United States. In 1900, in New Haven, Connecticut, Louis Lassen at his restaurant, Louis' Lunch, added 2 pieces of bread to the hamburg steak and the modern American hamburger was born. When the hamburger was shown at The St. Louis World Fair in 1904, the hamburger was on its way.

Happy Hour – Happy hour is a set period of time, often between 4 pm and 6 pm, when drinks and bar food have reduced prices to bring customers in during slow weekdays.

The term comes from the US Navy in the 1920s when time was set aside for "Happy Hour" when sailors could relax with sports or music to fight boredom. Later, during prohibition, the term happy hour came to mean having a few drinks at home before going to a restaurant where drinking was illegal.

Several states hate happy hour because they believe it encourages binge drinking. Currently, happy hour is prohibited in eight US states: Massachusetts, Alaska, Indiana, North Carolina, Oklahoma, Rhode Island, Utah, and Vermont and several countries.

Internationally, happy hour has been banned in Ireland and restrictions have been put in place in the rest of the UK in an effort to curtail binge drinking. In Canada even the term "Happy Hour" is prohibited.

Harvey Wallbanger (vodka, orange juice, Galliano Italian liqueur). Some say it was named for Tom Harvey, a California surfer, who would literally bang into walls when he would have this drink. Others say it was invented by bartender Donato Antone of Duke's Blackwatch Bar in California. The drink became popular when Galliano used it in its ads.

Heimlich maneuver – used when a person is choking. Henry Heimlich (1920-2016, born in Wilmington, Delaware) was credited with inventing the maneuver in 1972. He first called it "subdiaphragmatic pressure," but the editors of the Journal of the American Medical Association wanted to name the procedure after him. Thankfully, the editors won.

Ice Box: The first ice refrigerator (icebox) was patented in 1803.

Irish Coffee – Irish Coffee was created in the winter of 1943 by Joe Sheridan, chef at Foynes airbase near Limerick, Ireland. Foynes airbase was a stopover for longer flights to refuel and stay the night if bad weather.

One evening, a flight had to turn back to Foynes Air base midway through its journey. Wanting to warm the passengers, Joe decided to make something special for them to drink. The story goes that the name came about with the following exchange:

"Hey Buddy," said a surprised American passenger, "is this Brazilian coffee?" "No," said Joe, "this is *Irish* coffee." The Buena Vista Café in San Francisco is said to have introduced Irish coffee in the United States in 1952.

Kiva Han – The first coffee house in the world opened in Constantinople in 1475. It took only 177 years for London to get its first coffeehouse in 1652. But they made up for it in a big way since, just 10 years later, 3,000 coffeehouses were in and around London.

Knife, Spoon and Fork – The knife and fork have been around for a very long time. The knife was the first human tool while the spoon was used by the ancient Greeks. The fork is actually the new kid on the dining block. In the 11th century, forks were used in the Byzantine Empire, but they had only 2 prongs and mainly used for spearing food from a serving plate. The modern fork with 4 tines didn't make it to widespread use to get food from the plate to the mouth until the late 1600's and early 1700's. The whole design of the fork evolved. The end of the prongs was softened to avoid injuring the tongue when putting the fork in the mouth making it much easier to pick up the food. The increase in the number of prongs, from 2, then 3, then finally settling in at 4, plus the reduction of space between the prongs, made the fork a better option than the spoon for non-liquid foods. Eating with just a knife was considered vulgar, but Americans continued to use the knife until the early 1900's.

Mai tai – 1944 – Chef Victor Bergeron invented the Mai Tai at Trader Vic's.

Margarita (tequila, orange liqueur, freshly squeezed lime juice, agave syrup with lime wheel and kosher salt rim). Some say it was invented in 1948 in Acapulco, Mexico, when a Dallas socialite combined tequila with Cointreau and lime juice. Others say that the Margarita, which translates to daisy flower in Spanish, was an inevitable twist on the Daisy, a cocktail using some liquor, citrus, orange liqueur and soda.

Martini – (gin, dry vermouth, bitters, olive or lemon twist garnish) First made in 1862 by San Francisco bartender Jerry Thomas for a customer who said he had to travel to the city of Martinez, he called the new drink the martini.

Michelin Guide – is published for the first time in 1911, continue until 1933 and restarted in 1974.

Mickey Finn has come to mean a drugged drink. There really was a Chicago bartender named Mickey Finn, who gave the drugged drink to people who he later robbed.

Milk shake mixer – included because Ray Kroc, maybe the most famous milk shake mixer salesman, would never have visited the McDonald brothers.

Mint julep – bourbon poured over crushed ice and garnished with mint leaves. 1809. It was widely believed to be protection against malaria.

Nachos – Chef Ignacio "Nacho" Anaya created the dish at the Victory Club in Piedras, Mexico in 1940.

Onion Rings – A & W Restaurants is usually credited with making this popular in the 1960's, although they were around in the 1920's. However, some say it was the Pig Stand chain that was the inventor, along with chicken-fried steak sandwiches and Texas Toast.

Oven Thermometer – London inventor, Thomas Masters invents the world's first oven thermometer in 1850 made out of glass and mercury.

Pizza – Originated in Naples, Italy where flat bread topped with tomatoes were a local favorite in the late 1700's. Love it or hate it, the Hawaiian pizza, topped with pineapple and ham, was first made in Canada in 1962.

Poor boys (po boys) – Sooo New Orleans. French bread loaf with shrimp, oyster, catfish, soft-shell crabs, fried eggplant, French fries, ham, and cheese. The term "poor boy" came from the 1929 streetcar strike when the owners of the Martin Brothers' French Market Restaurant and Coffee, Benny and Clovis Martin, wanted to help the strikers by providing food.

Potato skins – (1971ish) Restaurants found it difficult to predict how many baked potatoes would be needed each shift and usually cooked too many. What to do? Throw away? The horrors. Money wasted. Too few? Mad and disappointed customers. Someone, somewhere, had the brilliant solution that these baked potatoes could be transformed into appetizers by frying and then topping with cheese, bacon bits, chives, and sour cream. TGI Fridays, The Prime Rib Restaurant in DC, and R.J. Grunts in Chicago, have all been credited with originating potato skins.

Printed menu – The first printed menu in the US in 1836 by Delmonico's Restaurant, New York.

Refrigerator 1926. George Munters and Baltzar Carl von Platen (Sweden). The first actual refrigerator based on Munters and von Platen's work was made and sold by the Electrolux Refrigerator Sales Company.

The Restaurant Compendium for the Curious

Restaurant – The actual word "restaurant" comes from the early 19th century French word *restaurer* meaning to 'restore to a former state', 'to restore', or 'to revive'. France's first public restaurant (as opposed to an inn which served overnight guests or a tavern which was mostly drinking alcohol) opened in 1765 in Paris by Boulanger. France's first true restaurant opened in Paris in 1782 as the La Grande Taverne de Londres by Antoine de Beauvilliers. The restaurant had uniformed waiters and good wines.

Salisbury Steak – is basically a ground beef hamburger without the bun, flavored with onion and seasonings, and covered with gravy or a brown sauce. Named for J.H. Salisbury, an American doctor who prescribed it to his patients in 1888. Dr. Salisbury believed humans should eat more meat with limited veggies and suggested that the Salisbury steak be eaten three times per day with hot water. This became known as the Salisbury diet.

Salmonella – infected food produces gastroenteritis with fever. It got its name from Daniel Salmon, a US veterinarian with the Department of Agriculture who described the microorganisms.

Sandwich - named after John Montagu, the 4th Earl of Sandwich (1718–92). In 1762, Mr. or Sir Sandwich created the sandwich by having his servant bring him cold, thick pieces of roast beef between 2 pieces of toasted bread because he did not want to leave the gambling table.

Singapore Sling – Invented in 1915 at Singapore's Raffles Hotel. (gin, cherry brandy, Cointreau, orange, lemon, or pineapple juice, and Angostura bitters, with cherry or pineapple garnish.

Sit-Down Meals – In 1657, fire destroyed much of the city of Edo, Japan's capital city. This event caused food cart vendors to set up shops where customers could sit down and eat meals.

Stainless Steel: Works for food because it does not affect taste, is easily cleaned and sterilized, is durable, and does not rust, and is completely recyclable. Stainless steel's resistance to rusting is because of chromium in the alloy. In 1913, at the beginning of WW I, Harry Brearley of Sheffield, UK was trying to eliminate erosion of internal surfaces of gun barrels for the British army when he invented the first true stainless steel.

Tacos – The native Nahuatl people of Mexico ate fish in flat corn bread. In the 16th century, Spanish explorers gave the name tortillas and filled it with chicken and beef.

Tequila Sunrise (tequila, grenadine, fresh lime juice, soda) was created at the Biltmore Phoenix Hotel by bartender Gene Sulit in the 1930's.

Tom Collins (gin, lemon juice, simple syrup, club soda) was a London bartender who invented this in the 1800's.

Toilet Paper: (1857). Joseph C. Gayetty (US). It was marketed as "Gayetty's Medicated Paper."

Deeper Dive
The Ubiquitous Restaurant Dishwasher

Josephine Garis Cochrane (1839-1912) loved entertaining but hated that her china chipped after hand washings. In 1886, she built a prototype dishwasher using wire racks to hold the dishes in place, set the racks into a wooden wheel resting in a copper boiler filled with hot water with a crank or small motor turning a wheel splashing hot water onto the dishes. She obtained a patent, went into production, and showed her 'Cochrane Dishwasher' at the 1893 World's Columbian Exposition in Chicago where she won the highest prize for her design and construction. She started the Garis-Cochrane Manufacturing Company, which was bought by KitchenAid in 1926. She was posthumously inducted into the National Inventors Hall of Fame in 2006 for her invention of the dishwasher.

Restaurant Event Timeline –
Significant and some not so much

2000 BC Forks made from bones found in Gansu, China

AD 1 Apicius writes the world's first cookbook, "De Re Coquinaria" ("On Cookery")

AD 300s Forks in common use in the Eastern Roman Empire

AD 400 Chinese chopsticks (eating sticks) used as eating utensils

11th Century Forks in use in the Byzantine Empire

1100 First identifiable restaurants appeared in China

1475 The world's first coffeehouse, Kiva Han, opens in Constantinople

1500s Tempura starts in Japan

1518 Forks first mentioned as used during meals in Venice

1680 Legend has it that the Benedictine monk, Dom Perignon, first used cork in wine bottles

1680s Gunsmiths modified musket barrel cleaning tools to work as a corkscrew. A musket barrel cleaning tool was known as a gun worm while the wine corkscrew was known as a steel worm

1700s The cocktail is invented in New York, USA. The original cocktail was a mixture of spirit, bitters, sugar, and water with bitters being the ingredient that makes a cocktail a cocktail

1700s The fork as we know it with 4 tines becomes the standard

1762 Sandwich is invented in London's Beef Steak Club, where John Montagu, fourth earl of Sandwich, he spent 24 hours gambling and does not want to leave the table

1785 Joseph Bramah patents the first beer tap, called a "beer engine."

Before this, beer was poured directly from the barrel, then carried to the customer

1793 The chef's toque is introduced so that the chef could be seen anywhere in the kitchen

1793 Julien's Restorator, the US's first French restaurant opens in the United States. Some say it is also the first real restaurant in the US (Jean Baptiste Gilbert Payplat dis Julien)

1803 The first refrigerator (icebox) is patented

1803 The world's first restaurant guide is published. "Almanach des Gourmands"2 by Alexandre Balthasar Laurent

1830s Fried potatoes (Pomme Frites or French fries) first become popular in France and Belgium

1831 Delmonico's Restaurant opens in New York City. Possibly the first modern-day restaurant in the United States. The first to use tablecloths, created the Delmonico steak, eggs Benedict, Baked Alaska, and Lobster Newburg. (John and Peter Delmonico). Delmonico's pastry shop opened in 1827. Original Delmonico's closes in 1923

1834 America's first printed menu is used in Delmonico's Restaurant in New York

1838 Gas ovens installed at London's Reform Club

1849 Tadich Grill opens in San Francisco (still open)

1849 The first Chinese restaurant in the United States, Macao and Woosung, opens in San Francisco. Some say they first created chop suey

1850 The oven thermometer is invented in London by Thomas Masters

1857 First Greek restaurant, Peloponnesos, opens in New York City

1850s First Italian Restaurant, Caffe Moretti, opens in the United

States in New York City

1860 First fish and chips restaurant opens at Tommyfield Market in Oldham, England

1866 The urinal is patented by Andrew Rankin. During the industrial revolution when factories hired many men, the urinal required less space in bathrooms. In France, urinals are called pissoirs and were introduced in Paris in the 1900s

1866 Charles Goodnight invents the Chuck Wagon, possibly the first food truck

1874 The Spork (combination of spoon and fork) patented by Samuel Francis

1879 The Boston Cooking School opens as the first cooking school in the United States

1880 L'Ecole de Cordon Bleu is founded in Paris by cooking teacher Marthe Distel

1880 Japan passes a law making it a criminal offense to sell food or drink that would be hazardous to health.

1885 Salmonella bacteria gets its name from the author of a paper on microorganisms that produces gastroenteritis with fever when infected food is eaten. The author is Daniel Elmer Salmon

1889 First Japanese restaurant opens in New York City

1893 Maxim's opens in Paris. The owner is Maxime Gaillard who dropped the e

1900 The Michelin Guide is first published in Paris

1902 The beginning of fast food in America arrives with the opening of the Horn and Hardart automat in New York City, New York (Joseph Horn and James Hardart)

1904 The St. Louis World's Fair introduces the hamburger to the world

1905 The first pizzeria, Lombardi's Pizza, opens in New York

1916 The end of common usage of the finger bowl, used to cleanse the fingers after a fruit or shellfish course

1918 The Pitco Frialator was invented which went on to become a restaurant fixture

1918 For the first time, more food consumed in restaurants than at home

1918 Restaurants put glass on tabletops to save linen and laundry during WW I

1919 The first airline meal (pre-packed lunch boxes) was served on a Handley-Page Transport flight (modified WW I bomber) from a flight from London to Paris

1919 The National Restaurant Association holds its first convention in Kansas City, Missouri

1920 Prohibition begins on January 16 with the 18th amendment

1921 One of the first drive-in restaurants, The Pig Stand, opens in Dallas, Texas (Jessie Kirby).

1921 The first hamburger chain, White Castle Hamburgers, opens in Wichita, Kansas (Billy Ingram). In 1925, they changed their look to a brick building with white enamel on the outside and white porcelain on the inside to emphasize cleanliness

1922 Cornell University opens the first undergraduate hospitality management university program

1923 Economics Laboratory (Ecolab) opens with a carpet cleaning product

1924 Stouffer restaurant chain starts as the Stouffer Lunch (Mahala Stouffer and her husband, Abraham) in Cleveland, Ohio. Their son, a Wharton School of Business graduate, joins his parents

1924 A&W Root Beer is the first restaurant to franchise. JW Marriott is one of the first A&W franchisees (in 1927)

1926 Route 66 opens, bringing opportunities for restaurants all along the route

1928 One of the world's greatest inventions, sliced bread, is actually invented

1928 Lufthansa Airlines serves the first hot meals in-flight

1929 American Culinary Federation (ACF) founded to support chefs and cooks

1931 Rolla Harger, a biochemist, invents the 'Drunkometer', the first successful test for blood alcohol content

1931 The Pig Stand No. 21, Dallas, Texas, becomes the first drive-*through* restaurant, rather than a drive-*in* (Jesse Kirby)

1933 Prohibition ends with the passing of the 21st amendment repealing the 18th amendment

1934 Wimpy's Hamburgers opens by an American, Edward Gold, in Bloomington, Indiana

1934 Muzak starts. Major General George Owen Squier (West Point graduate and PhD from Johns Hopkins University) liked the company name Kodak. He took the first three letters from the word "music," added the letters "ak" from Kodak, and Muzak was born

1935 Howard Johnson's restaurants begin to franchise

1936 40-hour work week and overtime begin. If employee worked over 40 hours, the employer had to pay 1.5 times the employee's hourly wage. This penalty was a great incentive for companies to hire more people and helped reduce unemployment during the Great Depression.

1936 United Airlines installs first on-board kitchens for hot meals

1936 Oscar Mayer's Weiner Mobile first appears

1936 Harland Sanders given the honorary title "Kentucky Colonel" by the governor of Kentucky.

1937 Victor Bergeron changes the décor of his lunch and beer parlor, Hinky Dinks, to a Polynesian décor and renames it Trader Vic's

1938 The new Federal minimum wage law guarantees workers 25 cents per hour

1939 First commercial pressure cookers available. Harland (Colonel) Sanders modifies it to be a pressure fryer for his chicken to speed up the 35-minute cooking times

1940 Richard and Maurice 'Mac' McDonald open a drive-in restaurant, McDonald's Bar-B-Q, in San Bernardino, California

1946 The first culinary college in the United States, The Culinary Institute of America is founded

1948 The McDonald brothers change McDonald's from drive-in carhop service to self-service

1950 Diners Club Card starts when businessman Frank McNamara forgot his wallet at a New York City restaurant. Diners Club is founded to give credit card privileges at a group of 27 New York area restaurants. In its first year of business, Diners Club® grew to 10,000 members with 28 restaurants and two hotels accepting monthly billing

1950 Federal minimum wage raises to $0.75 per hour

1952 KFC begins franchising with first franchisee in Salt Lake City, Utah

1953 Denny's opens as Danny's Donuts (Danny with an a), in Lakewood, California. 1959 Changes name to Denny's Coffee Shops. Name changes to just Denny's in 1961

1953 The first dinner theater opens in Richmond, Virginia (David and Nancy Kilgore)

1954 Burger King opens in Miami, Florida (James McLamore and David Edgerton). In 1953, Burger King was started as Insta-Burger King

1954 Britain's first Wimpy hamburger starts in London, England. Wimpy is the name of the character in Popeye comics who loves hamburgers. See 1934.

1955 Federal minimum wage raised to $1.00 per hour

1955 Ray Kroc opens his first McDonald's franchise in Des Plaines, Illinois, the 21st McDonald's franchise

1957 Burger King Whopper is introduced

1958 American Express Card starts

1959 Chada Thai, opens in Denver, Colorado as the first Thai restaurant in the US

1961 Ray Kroc buys out the McDonald brothers for $2.7 million

1961 McDonald's establishes Hamburger University in Elk Grove, Illinois. Graduates receive a bachelor in hamburgerology and a minor in French fries

1961 First Vietnamese restaurant in the US opens in New York City

1961 Federal minimum wage raised to $1.15 per hour

1963 The one billionth McDonald's hamburger is served by Ray Kroc on the Art Linkletter Show

1963 "The French Chef" airs on PBS with Julia Child becoming the first celebrity chef

1963 Federal minimum wage raised to $1.25 per hour

1964 Benihana of Tokyo opens in New York City (Hiroaki 'Rocky' Aoki). Benihana means Red Flower in Japanese

1966 The salad bar is popularized by Steak and Ale

1966 The infamous words "Hi, I'm Billy, and I'll be your waiter" is first enthusiastically spoken at Steak and Ale in Dallas, Texas

1966 First Ethiopian restaurant in America, The Ethiopian Restaurant, opens in Long Beach, California

1966 The Fair Labor Standards Act (FLSA) includes tip credit allowing employers to pay half of the prevailing minimum wage as long as their employee's tips make up the difference

1967 McDonald's test markets the Big Mac (originally named the Aristocrat, then the Blue-Ribbon burger, then mercifully, Big Mac)

1971 Salmagundi opens its first location in San Francisco, California (David Hugle and Todd Jenkins)

1971 First Starbucks (only sold coffee beans) opens in Seattle, Washington (Jerry Baldwin, Zev Siegl and Gordon Bowker)

1974 Federal minimum wage raised to $2.00 per hour

1975 Federal minimum wage raised to $2.10 per hour

1975 McDonald's opens its first drive-thru in Arizona

1975 Anchor Brewing launches Liberty Ale, America's first modern IPA

1976 Nachos first comes to the general public at Arlington Stadium where the Texas Rangers baseball team played (Frank Liberto's company, Liberto Specialty Company)

1976 Federal minimum wage raised to $2.30 per hour

1977 McDonald's begins full breakfast menu

1977 Denny's begins The Grand Slam breakfast in honor of Hank Aaron

1978 Federal minimum wage raised to $2.65 per hour

1979 Federal minimum wage raised to $2.90 per hour

1980 Zagat New York City begins (Timothy and Nina Zagat)

1980 The deadliest fire in Nevada's history, resulting in 87 deaths and 650 injured occurred at the Deli restaurant in the MGM Grand Hotel and Casino

1980 The first Applebee's restaurant, T.J. Applebee's Rx for Edibles &

Elixirs, opens in Atlanta, Georgia. In 1986, name was changed to Applebee's Neighborhood Grill & Bar (Bill and T.J. Palmer)

1980 Federal minimum wage raised to $3.10 per hour

1981 Federal minimum wage raised to $3.35 per hour

1982 TV show "Cheers" begins

1982 Bud Light introduced by Anheuser-Busch

1982 "Foodie" becomes a thing

1983 Bert Grant's Yakima Brewing and Malting Company has the first beer to be labeled IPA in Yakima, Washington

1983 The "breastaurant" genre of restaurants begins with Hooters opening in Clearwater, Florida.

1986 Carlo Perini founds the Slow Food Organization in Italy

1987 KFC becomes the first western restaurant chain to open in China

1987 Howard Schultz buys Starbucks, a Seattle coffee bean business, and begins to open Starbucks coffee locations. Schultz already owned a chain of coffee shops called Il Giornale which he converted and renamed Starbucks

1988 New York City enacts law requiring restaurants with 50 seats or more to provide separate sections for smokers and nonsmokers

1990 Federal minimum wage raised to $3.80 per hour

1990 San Luis Obispo, California becomes the first city in the world to ban indoor smoking in restaurants and bars

1991 McDonald's opens in Moscow with more than 50,000 customers per day

1991 Federal minimum wage raised to $4.25 per hour

1991 Kentucky Fried Chicken changes name to KFC for two reasons: to get rid of the word fried and because the state of Kentucky trademarked "Kentucky" requiring any use of its name for business pur-

Trivia and the Small Stuff

poses meant paying royalty payments to the state of Kentucky

1993 The Food Network starts

1994 Ad Age awards Chili's restaurants jingle "Baby back , baby back ribs" the number one song "most likely to get stuck in your head"

1996 Federal minimum wage raised to $4.75 per hour

1997 Federal minimum wage raised to $5.15 per hour

1997 Restaurant Nora in Washington, DC becomes the first certified organic restaurant in the United States (Nora Pouillon)

1997 Revised federal tip credit allows employers to pay eligible tipped employees $2.13 per hour if they receive the remainder of the statutory minimum wage in tips

1998 California becomes first state to ban smoking in restaurants and bars

1998 OpenTable begins taking online restaurant reservations. Went public in 2009 (OPEN). (Chuck Templeton)

1998 Britain enacts its first minimum wage of £3.60 an hour for adults 22 and older and £3.00 for 18-21. Went into effect in 1999

1999 The US Department of Commerce declares this "the year of the Restaurant"

2001 Because of the September 11th attacks, airlines begin to use plastic silverware

2003 MySpace launches becoming the largest social media site in the world

2004 Facebook is founded (Mark Zuckerberg, Eduardo Saverin, Andrew McCollom, Dustin Moskovitz, and Chris Hughes)

2006 The Hard Rock Cafes and Casinos are purchased by Florida's Seminole American Indian Tribe

2007 Federal Minimum wage raised to $5.85 per hour

2007 Domino's Pizza first pizza company to have cell phone ordering

2008 Federal Minimum wage raised to $6.55 per hour

2008 All 7,100 US Starbucks Coffee Shops close for 3 hours of employee training

2009 Gourmet magazine shuts down

2009 Federal Minimum wage set at $7.25 per hour. Last increase as of 2022

2012 Rebekah Speight of Dakota City, Nebraska sold a McDonald's Chicken McNugget that resembled President George Washington for $8,100 on eBay

2012 Japan Airlines serves KFC chicken during the Christmas holidays

2013 DoorDash, originally called PaloAltoDelivery.com, begins in Palo Alto, California (Tony Xu, Stanley Tang, Andy Fang, and Evan Moore)

2014 Uber Eats is founded

2015 Danny Meyer, founder and CEO of Union Square Hospitality Group, starts to phase out tipping

2016 New York and California pass laws raising minimum wages to $15 per hour

2017 France bans restaurants from offering free refills of sodas and other sugary drinks

2019 December 8, the first known case of COVID-19 traced to Wuhan, China

2020 On January 20, Center for Disease Control (CDC) confirms first case of COVID-19 in US in the state of Washington.

2020 March 13, US declares COVID-19 national emergency

2020 On March 15, the first restaurants in US close because of COVID-19 when Ohio Governor Mike DeWine ordered restaurants and bars closed. Within days, other states followed

2020 By March 23, an estimated 7 million restaurant and bar employees are unemployed

2020 During last half of 2020, sales at quick-service restaurants exceeds 2019 during the same period, but full-service restaurants still down 25%.

2021 The National Restaurant Association reports that in mid year, there were over 1.7 million restaurant job openings

2022 For the first time since pre-pandemic, sales are expected to surpass 2019

US Trends Over the Decades

1910s
(Immigration, WW I, Hyphenated decade)

Estimated that for the first time, more food eaten out in restaurants than at home. During the war years (1914-1918), restaurants placed glass on tabletops to save on laundry. **Italian-American, Chinese-American, and Jewish-American foods appear in restaurants, such as spaghetti and meatballs, chop suey, chow mein, Swedish meatballs,** vichyssoise (also called leek and potato soup), **and goulashes** popular along with other ethnic foods.

1920s
(Roaring Twenties, Prohibition)

Cafeterias, luncheonettes, tea rooms, speakeasies. As automobiles become more common, restaurant owners worry that drivers won't see their restaurants, so they build novelty architecture restaurants, like the Bulldog Café in Los Angeles. Fast food begins with the opening of the first White Castle restaurant. Finger foods begin with oyster cocktails, shrimp patties, and pimiento stuffed mushrooms. Caesar salad, the cobb salad, and green goddess salad dressing all contributed to making salads not just a "girly" thing.

1930s
(The Great Depression, end of Prohibition)

All-you-can-eat and soda shops are everywhere. Congealed and Jell-O salads and devilled eggs make their debut. One pot meals, meat loaf, mac and cheese, and casseroles are developed to make meals go further. The Joy of Cooking cookbook is released.

1940s
(World War 2 and post war)

Women are in the workplace in record numbers causing restaurant popularity to rise. The chiffon cake becomes popular, invented by the baker (Henry Baker!) at Brown Derby restaurant.

1950s
(Post WW II booming boomer economy with fast food and pizza)

For first time in history, teens have economic power. Polynesian tiki culture fad hits the US with Don the Beachcomber and Trader Vic's, even though they both opened in the 1930s. Drive-in restaurants become popular. Restaurants open along interstate highways and population moves to the suburbs. California dip, fish sticks, and sloppy joes arrive. Because of the explosion of fast-food restaurants with its assembly line production, low skilled employees have more opportunity.

1960s
(Cold war, astronauts, protests, Vietnam war, casual family restaurants)

For the first time, dinner becomes more about family time, not just eating to live. Restaurants introduce salad bars, surf and turf, shrimp cocktails, Swedish meatballs, fern bars, and theme restaurants. Freeze-dried astronaut foods, like freeze-dried ice cream becomes popular. Julia Child has enormous influence on restaurant dishes (eggs, cream, butter) like Coq au Vin. Buffalo wings is first introduced. Vegetarian restaurants with veggie chili, gazpacho, and zucchini bread become mainstream.

1970s
(The Me decade)

Dinner theaters everywhere. Healthy foods starting to influence restaurant menus more. Vegetarian options added to menus. Explosion of casual theme dining chains. Fondue and fondue restaurants expand. Brunch takes off with restaurants. Alice Waters' Chez Panisse has enormous influence on chefs with natural, local, and seasonal ingredients, with arugula, not iceberg lettuce.

1980s
(Decade of excess)

Growth of celebrity chef inspired foods. Nouvelle cuisine found in fine dining restaurants. Paul Prudhomme causes Cajun cooking to explode with blackened fish and everything else. IPA beers are introduced nationwide. Wine coolers introduced. Towering food sculptures (Timbales) are introduced. Frozen yogurt shops explode and pasta primavera everywhere. Sushi and especially the California roll popular. Expensive olive oils and balsamic vinegars appear. Wolfgang Puck becomes household name. Tex-Mex food takes hold.

1990s
(World Wide Web)

"Breastaurant" category begins with the opening of Hooters, later joined by Redneck Heaven, The Tilted Kilt, and Twin Peaks. Fusion cooking (blending different cultural dishes) becomes a fad, but to some it was just "con-fusion." Growth of microbreweries with pubs, gastro pubs, and restaurants adding craft beers. The number of coffee shops explodes with some crediting the TV show "Friends," (with its setting in the Central Perk coffee house) as helping accelerate coffee shops' growth; much like the TV show "Loveboat" ignited the cruise industry. Starbucks goes from 425 units in 1994 to 3,501 by the end of 1999.

Cyber/Internet cafes open all over the world in the early 1990s. Sun-dried tomatoes, fat-free, and focaccia everywhere. The term "molecular gastronomy" was born.

2000s
(Along comes healthy)

Healthy foods along with an interest in food sources, like local produce. Morgan Spurlock's 2004 documentary "Super-Size Me" has an enormous influence on fast food menus. Foods like sushi and super fruits, blueberries and Acai berries, popular in restaurants, but to balance healthy, there is bacon flavored everything. Cupcakes huge. The book, 'Dr. Atkins' Diet Revolution: The High Calorie Way to Stay Thin Forever' is enormously popular in the early 2000s with its low carb/high protein diet affecting restaurant menus.

2010s
(Craft, small batch, curated)

Craft breweries reach over 5,000 in the US in 2016, according to the Brewers Association. Guacamole and sliders popular in bar menus. Instagram starts in 2010 and photos of restaurant food everywhere. Food trucks roll. "Sustainable," "artisanal," and "locavore" are added to vocabulary and menus.

2020s
(COVID-19 pandemic: labor shortages, supply chain problems, masks, and shutdowns)

COVID-19 pandemic dominates as the major influencer. Drive-thrus, take-out, and food delivery become essential for restaurant survival. "Contactless" becomes a thing. The rise of third-party delivery services, like Grub Hub, Uber Eats, and locals become essential. Ghost kitchens, cloud kitchens, dark kitchens, and virtual kitchens become increasingly important to restaurants. Pandemic leads to many industries able to work from home, but not restaurants. Sustainable food movement grows. Restaurants turning to technology and robotics to combat labor shortages. Employees demand more pay and benefits; unions start to join the conversation.

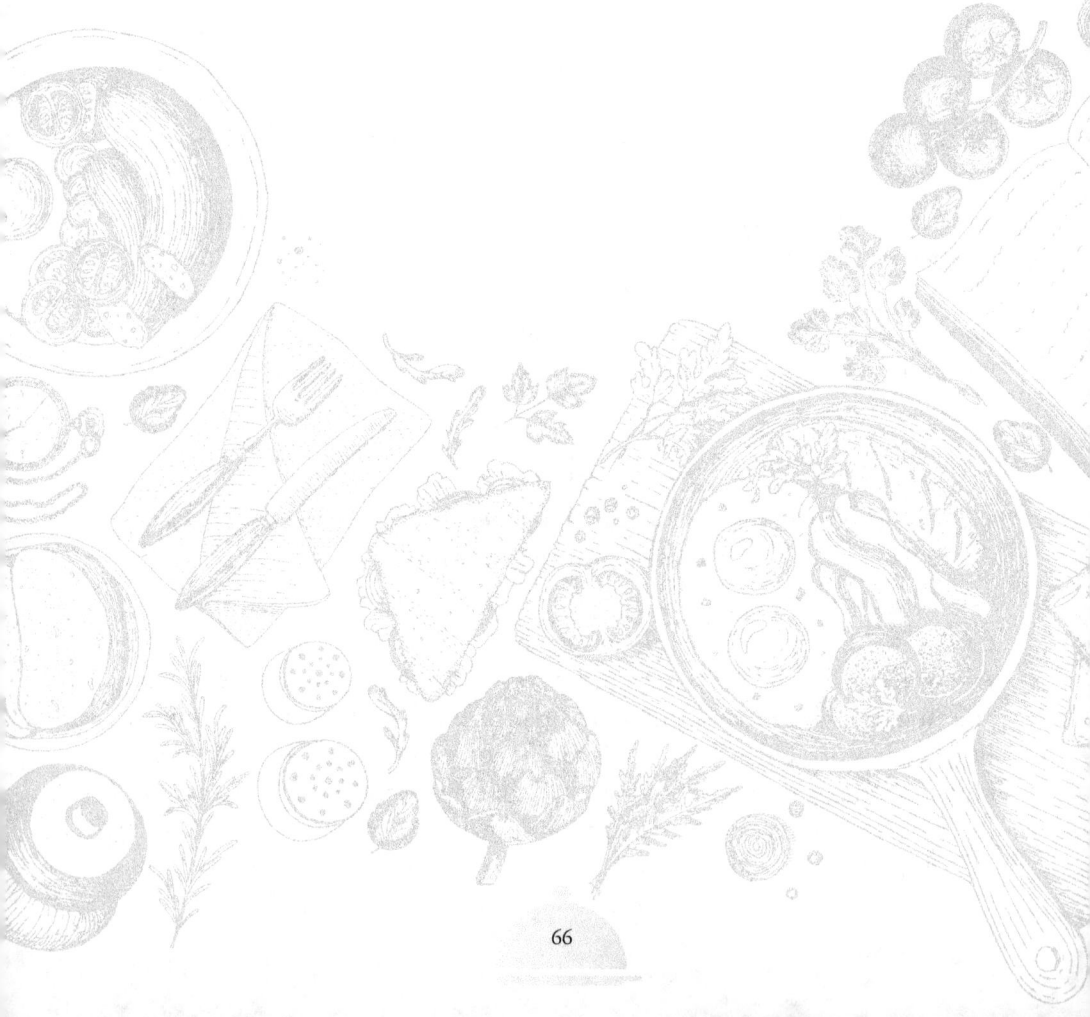

Holidays Celebrating Restaurants, Foods, and Drinks

January
Be Kind to Food Servers Month

Jan 1 National Bloody Mary Day
Jan 1 National Hangover Day
Jan 1 California Restaurant Month
Jan 2 National Buffet Day
Jan 4 National Spaghetti Day
Jan 7 National Tempura Day
Jan 10 National Oysters Rockefeller Day
Jan 11 National Hot Toddy Day
Jan 12 National Curried Chicken Day
Jan 14 National Hot Pastrami Sandwich Day
Jan 15 National Bagel Day
Jan 18 National Peking Duck Day
Jan 23 National Pie Day
Jan 25 National Irish Coffee Day
Jan 27 National Chocolate Cake Day
Jan 28 National Blueberry Pancake Day
Jan 30 National Croissant Day

February
National Fasting February and National Hot Breakfast month

February 6 Super Chicken Wing Day
February 7 National Fettuccine Alfredo Day
February 9 National Pizza Day
Feb 13 National Tortellini Day
Feb 18 National Drink Wine Day
Feb 22 National Margarita Day

March
National Noodle Month

March 1 International Pancake Day
Mar 2 National Egg McMuffin Day
Mar 5 National Absinthe Day
Mar 14 Pi Day
Mar 27 International Whiskey Day

April
National Garlic Month

April 4 National Cordon Bleu Day
April 7 National Beer Day
April 17 Malbec World Day
April 27 National Prime Rib Day
April 29 National Shrimp Scampi Day

May
National Barbeque Month

May 5 National Enchilada Day
May 9 National Shrimp Day
May 10 National Liver and Onions Day
May 13 National Apple Pie Day
May 16 National Barbecue Day
May 25 National Wine Day
May 28 National Brisket Day

June
National Soul Food Month

June 2 National Rotisserie Chicken Day
June 12 International Falafel Day
June 15 Lobster Day

June 19 National Martini Day
June 22 National Onion Ring Day
June 22 – National Onion Rings Day
June 25 National Catfish Day
June 30 National Mai Tai Day

July
National Culinary Arts Month

July 4 Caesar Salad Day
July 6 National Fried Chicken Day
July 10 National Pina Colada Day
July 11 National Mojito Day
July 13 National French Fry Day
July 24 National Tequila Day
July 27 National Scotch Day
July 28 National Hamburger Day
July 29 National Chicken Wing Day

August
National Eat Dessert First Month

August 3 National IPA Day
August 8 International Beer Day
August 13 National Filet Mignon Day
August 16 National Rum Day
August 27 National Burger Day

September
All American Breakfast Month

September 3 National Baby Back Ribs Day
September 5 National Cheese Pizza Day
September 7 National Beer Lover's Day
September 16 National Guacamole Day
September 18 National Cheeseburger Day

October
Eat Better, Eat Together Month

October 1 World Vegetarian Day
October 3 National Soft Taco Day
October 4 National Taco Day
October 4 National Vodka Day
October 12 National Gumbo Day and Pumpkin Pie Day
October 17 National Pasta Day
October 25 National Greasy Foods Day

November

November 1 World Vegan Day
November 5 National Chinese Take-out Day
November 6 National Nachos Day
November 8 National Cappuccino Day
November 12 National Pizza With The Works Except Anchovies Day
November 16 National Fast-Food Day
November 23 National Espresso Day

December

December 1 National Pie Day
December 5 Repeal of Prohibition Day
December 29 National "Get On the Scales" Day

Chapter II

FUNNY STUFF

 # JOKES

Me and the girlfriend went to a restaurant.
The manager said, "I'm sorry, but we're so busy tonight. Would you mind waiting for a bit?"
I said, "No problem."
He said, "Great. Take these drinks to table 5."

How many line cooks does it take to screw in a lightbulb? Three. One to do it, and two to say that their previous restaurant did it better.

I went to a restaurant that serves "breakfast any time" so I ordered French toast during the Renaissance. ~ Steven Wright

A sandwich walked into a bar and sat down. The bartender said, "Sorry, we don't serve food here."

Two men are walking their dogs (a Doberman and a chihuahua) when they see a restaurant.
They're pretty hungry, so they decide to head in for a bite to eat. Unfortunately, they see a sign out front that says, "NO DOGS ALLOWED."
The man with the Doberman says, "I know what to do, just follow my lead." He throws on a pair of sunglasses and walks in.
The waiter tells him "I'm sorry sir, we don't allow dogs here."
The man says "Oh, you don't understand. I'm blind and this is my guide dog."
"A Doberman for a guide dog?" The waiter asks, skeptical.
"Yes." The man replies. "Dobermans are very loyal. They're easy to train and protective too. They're born for the job."
The waiter sighs and leads the man to a table.
The second man, excited by this idea, throws on his sunglasses and walks in.
The waiter tells him "I'm sorry sir, we don't allow dogs here."

The man says "Oh, you don't understand. I'm blind and this is my guide dog."
"A chihuahua for a guide dog?" the waiter asks.
"A chihuahua?" the man asks. "They gave me a chihuahua?!"

A guy sits at a bar in a skyscraper restaurant high above the city. He slams a shot of tequila, goes over to the window and jumps out.

The guy sitting next to him can't believe what he just saw. He's more surprised when, 10 minutes later, the same guy walks back into the bar and sits down next to him.

The astonished onlooker asks, "How did you do that? I just saw you jump out the window, and we're hundreds of feet above the ground!"

The jumper responds by slurring, "Well, I don't get it either. I slam a shot of tequila, and when I jump out the window, the tequila makes me slow down right before I hit the ground. Watch." He takes a shot, goes to the window and jumps out.

The other guy runs to the window and watches as the guy falls to just above the sidewalk, slows down and lands softly on his feet. A few minutes later, the jumper walks back into the bar.

The other guy has to try it, too, so he orders a shot of tequila. He slams it and jumps out the window. As he reaches the bottom, he doesn't slow down at all. SPLAT!

The first guy orders another shot of tequila. The bartender shakes his head. "You're really an ass when you're drunk, Superman."

My girlfriend is 22 and I'm 29. We go out to eat in a restaurant but the entire time I had to deal with being called disgusting and disturbed. It completely ruined our 10-year anniversary

Merlot has the distinction of being both easy to drink and pronounce.

Three ex-restaurant owners are having coffee. One says, "I had a fire, and the insurance took care of me." The second said, "I had a fire in my restaurant too. The insurance was great and really took care of me." The third said, "I had a flood in mine and the insurance was there for me."

The others looked at him and asked. "How did you start the flood?"

Groaners

A man is dining in a fancy restaurant. There is a gorgeous redhead sitting at the next table. He has been checking her out since he sat down but lacks the nerve to talk with her.

Suddenly she sneezes, and her glass eye comes flying out of its socket toward the man. He reaches out, grabs it out of the air, and hands it back.

'Oh my, I'm so sorry,' the woman says as she pops her eye back in place.

'Let me buy your dinner to make it up to you,' she says.

They enjoy a wonderful dinner together, and afterwards they go to the theatre followed by drinks. They talk, they laugh, she shares her deepest dreams, and he shares his. She listens.

After paying for everything, she asks him if he would like to come to her place for a nightcap and stay for breakfast. They have a wonderful, wonderful time.

The next morning, she cooks a gourmet breakfast. The guy is amazed. Everything had been so incredible!

'You know,' he said, 'you are the perfect woman. Are you this nice to every guy you meet?'

'No,' she replies. . . 'You just happened to catch my eye.'

I went to a cannibal restaurant last night... Very expensive...$200 a head

Did you know that Peter Pan had a brother named 'Deep'?

Two cannibals were eating a comedienne. One of the cannibals asked the other: "Does this taste funny to you?"

Why didn't the restaurant have urinals?
It was a sit-down restaurant

If you're waiting for the waiter at a restaurant, aren't you the waiter?

My wife and I have the secret to making a marriage last. Two times a week, we go to a nice restaurant and have wine and great food.

She goes on Tuesdays; I go on Fridays.

Double Groaners

Man asks waitress, "Pardon me miss, may I ask you about the menu please?"

Waitress, "It's none of your business about the men I please!"

Hear about the restaurant called karma? There's no menu. You get what you deserve.

Restaurant Management and Employee Placement Test

Take all restaurant applicants into a room with only a table, 2 chairs, pencils, and pens. Leave them alone for 2 hours without any instructions. At the end of 2 hours, go back and see what they are doing. Depending upon what they are doing at the end of 2 hours, this is how you've assigned them. The choices were Busser, Cashier, Chef, Dishwasher, Cook, Hostess, Server, Bartender, Owner, and Trainer.

The one who took the table apart
Busser

The one who counted the pencils and pens
Cashier

The one who is screaming and waving their arms
Chef

The one who is talking to the chairs
Dishwasher

The one who is sleeping
Manager

The one who is writing up the experience
Trainer

The one who doesn't even look up as you come into the room
Cook

The one who tells you it isn't as bad as it looks
Hostess

The one who tells you how screwed up this whole thing is
Server

The one who tells you that they don't need a placement test
Bartender

The one who left early
Owner

Funny Stuff

Shifts from hell
or
You think you've had a bad day?

**Everyone in restaurants have had a shift from hell.
Here are two of mine that I'll never forget**

#2

I was the general manager, and it was Memorial Day. I had decided that I would work this holiday, giving my assistants a much deserved (and rare) holiday off.

I researched the past two year's Memorial Day sales and the past two years were s l o w. So, I staffed for it to be slow. I let off as many as I thought I could spare so they could enjoy the holiday. A female manager in training in her last phase of training was scheduled to work this shift, so I knew that if I really needed some extra help somewhere, she could help.

I know you can tell where this is heading.

So, sure enough, it started out slow. Really slow. I was in the kitchen talking with my cooks when a server got my attention. He said the hostess was not seating him, but other servers were being seated.

I said OK, I'll be right there.

As I approached the hostess stand, I could see what looked like a couple of hundred people standing around the young hostess, all trying to get her attention. When I got to the hostess, I could see that she was softly crying, and was basically paralyzed, not doing anything. She was trying to put people on a waiting list but crying as she just stood there, pen in hand. Then I looked beyond the hostess and there were more people in the lobby crowding around.

Being the very sharp, quick, and astute manager that I was, I thought: This is not good.

No problem. I'll get my manager trainee.

But, not so fast, grasshopper. That was when it went from not good to very bad.

The bar was packed, every seat at every table sat. I looked at the manager trainee as she was taking an order. She too was crying as she was bravely taking drink orders.

So gotta do something. What to do. What to do.

With nothing to lose, I gathered up the first four groups in the lobby and sat them in the first four tables. I continued to do this until the lobby was clear. Then I started in the bar until all my servers were maxed out. I figured the servers could be trusted to bust their butts and do at least a pretty good job with my help.

I then ran into the kitchen alerting the cooks that they were about to get slammed. My hostess recovered enough to help as did the manager trainee. Together we helped the servers as much as we could. After the servers went through their turn of chaos, the kitchen went through their chaos, so I switched to the kitchen to help as much as possible.

All in all, a really suck evening. I was physically and emotionally wiped out. I thought about saving all the customers some time by giving each customer my name and the name of my supervisor so they would know who to complain to. I thought about it, but I didn't.

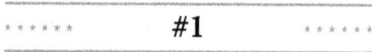

#1

Have you ever had one of those days when everything went wrong and all you wanted to do was go home, grab a beer, turn on the TV, watch anything, and just unwind?

Here we go.

The story begins on a Friday night…the restaurant was busy as hell, lines out the door, but it was going ok. No serious problems, except that we were a little shorthanded, so I had to buzz around quite a bit. I was really looking forward for the night to end. It was about a half hour before closing when I got a frantic tugging at my arm that the toilets had overflowed.

No problem. No big deal. I grabbed a busser, sent him in to clean it up, and forgot about it.

Then I got a report from the kitchen that the kitchen drains were all backing up and it was really getting wet in there. I go into the kitchen and sure enough, the floor was wet with water coming in through the drain lines. Lots of it. Fast. Did I say lots? Time for the plumber. I needed professional help now.

The water continued to rise. It didn't take long for the kitchen to be under 1 inch of water, then 2 inches. By now the water was starting to leak out into the dining room. Did I mention that this wasn't just water, but sewage water? Oh, yeah. And you can imagine that the water did not smell exactly great either.

I was in the kitchen with a mop when a hostess comes in to say that she was starting to get lots of complaints about the smell. Would I do something, please? The kitchen was totally flooded now with everyone just about ankle deep. The only one who was enjoying himself was the dishwasher, who loved that everyone was smelling and looking like he usually smelled and looked.

I turned around to talk to the hostess, when I slipped. Right into the muck. I fell totally flat. About a 9.3 in the new Olympic event of manager-slipping-in sewage-in-kitchen. I was sopping wet, not feeling real good. I was wet, frustrated, and smelly.

I couldn't leave to change since I was the only manager. I put on a cook's shirt from the office, which was too small because we had just given out all the larger ones. But, it was clean, which meant it was fine, even though it was really tight and looked ridiculous on me.

The plumber arrived late of course. By the time the plumber had finished, and I had mopped the kitchen by myself, (I had sent everyone home because it was so late), I was totally beat. It was around 3:30 AM in the morning. I finally got in my car to head home.

Little did I know that this night was just starting.

I was driving home when I spotted two guys next to a car who were trying to get someone to stop to help them.

I stopped.

What the hell; misery loves company. They said they had run out of gas and asked if I could give them a ride to a gas station? Sure, hop in. I drove to an all-night gas station. While I waited in the car, they went in to get some gas and coffee. As we drove back to their car with the gas, a police car gets in back of me, turns on its lights, and starts the siren right behind me.

I stopped.

He pulls out his gun and yells: "Get out and spread 'em!" It turns out that while my boys were in the gas station, they were also robbing the place. The gas station guy called the police and here we are!

It took a while before I convinced the policeman that I was not part of this entire deal, that I had just tried to help the hitchhikers. The policeman said he had heard that one before, but the guys helped me and actually said the same thing. I then showed the policeman where I had picked them up by their (stolen) car.

I was finally allowed to go home. As I pulled into the garage, the paper was being delivered, the sun was coming up, and now a beer sounded much better than coffee.

Funny Stuff

Annoying!
What REALLY Annoys Restaurant Employees

- Switching tables without asking
- Calling to your server when they are with another table
- Saying you're ready to order and not being ready to order
- Not moving plates/glasses out of the way when food arrives
- Hearing "What's good here?"
- "I know it's not on the menu, but…"
- Can you split this bill 17 ways? At the end of the meal. Sure. No problem.
- Snapping your fingers to get server's attention
- Coming in 5 minutes before closing
- Asking to get something for free (You can hook me up, can't you?)
- Customers who treat restaurants like daycare, letting their kids run around
- Customers who don't even try to clean up after their children trashed the table ("It's ok, they get paid to clean it up")
- Complaining on Yelp after saying everything was great to the server
- Listening to all your allergies, illnesses, and problems
- Customers who ignore their server
- Customers who say "I know the owner"
- Adults who order off the kid's menu
- Customers who tell their servers "Surprise me!"
- Campers: Customers who sit for an hour after they have finished their meal. Usually with a full restaurant and wait.
- The one customer who thinks he is a standup comedian (You're not

that funny and besides, I've heard them all before)
- Server brings out food and everyone just looks at the plate with no one claiming it.
- Singing "Happy Birthday"
- Did I mention, singing "Happy Birthday"?

What REALLY Annoys Restaurant Customers

- Wobbling table
- Taking dirty plates but leaving the dirty silverware
- Manager Question: "Is everything OK?"
- Customer reply: "Is OK really what you're shooting for?"
- Too dark – if you need a flashlight, it just might be too dark
- Too bright–if you need sunglasses, it just might be too bright.
- Music so loud that it is impossible to have a conversation
- Two front entry doors but only one opens. The other is locked.
- Too friendly/too talkative/hovering waitstaff – I don't want/need to be your best friend
- Many open tables, but host wants to seat you next to the kitchen/bathroom/server station
- Synthetic napkins that do not absorb
- Server: Hi, I'm Billy, and I'm going to be your server.
- Customer reply: Hi, I'm John, and I'm going to be your customer.
- Constant upselling for each item ordered
- Restaurant too cold because the temperature is set for servers, not customers
- Not having hooks for purses while sitting at the bar

- Servers not knowing where each plate goes, bringing out the food and says, "Who has the pasta primavera"? This is called 'auctioning' food.

Chapter III

THE WORLD'S MOST SURPRISING, UNUSUAL, ODD, QUIRKY, WEIRD RESTAURANTS AND WHY WE LOVE THEM

USA

The Airplane Restaurant, Colorado Springs, Colorado, USA. **Why?** You're dining in a Boeing KC-97 Stratofreighter tanker full of aviation memorabilia.

Aquarium Restaurant, Denver, Colorado. Why? You're dining in an aquarium!

Beetle House NYC, NYC, New York and LA, California. **Why?** A year-round adult Halloween party complete with singers, sword swallowers, magicians, contortionists, and impersonators.

Blackout, dining in the dark. Las Vegas, Nevada, USA. **Why?** You'll dine in total darkness with a 7-course mystery meal.

The Bubble Room, Captiva Island, Florida. **Why?** Three story restaurant decorated with classic toys from the 1930's and 1940's with moving trains in all 3 stories. "It's always Christmas at the Bubble Room."

Biscuit Belly, Lexington and Louisville, KY, Indiana and Georgia. **Why?** Everything biscuits, even bonuts (biscuit holes)

Dick's Last Resort, multiple US cities **Why?** Known for its intentionally obnoxious staff

Fife & Drum, Concord, Massachusetts **Why?** Used as a culinary arts program for the inmates housed at the Northeastern Correctional Center.

Fritz's Railroad Restaurant, Shawnee, Kansas **Why?** Ceiling mounted train and train memorabilia

Harvey Washbangers, College Station, Texas **Why?** Eat. Drink. Do laundry.

Heart Attack Grill, Las Vegas, Nevada, USA. **Why?** Waitresses are nurses and customers are patients. Try the Octuple Bypass burger

The Restaurant Compendium for the Curious

with 9,000 calories.

Ichiran, New York City, New York **Why?** Resembles a traditional Japanese ramen shop

Jekyll & Hyde Club, Restaurant and Bar, New York City, New York, USA. **Why?** If you like to be entertained with spooky special effects and enjoy creatures interacting with you, you've come to the right place.

Lambert's Cafe, Missouri and Alabama. **Why?** If you want a dinner roll, they *throw* them at you. Really.

Lucky Cheng's, New York City, New York. **Why?** The first Chinese Restaurant & Bar where entire staff are exotic Asian drag queens and transgendered women.

The Magic Castle, Los Angeles, California. **Why?** It's all about the magic.

Ninja New York, New York City, New York. **Why?** Servers dressed in black martial arts costumes amid a 15th century Japanese feudal village.

Post Office Pies, Birmingham, Alabama **Why?** Located in an historic post office

Rattlesnake Saloon, Tuscumbia, Alabama. **Why?** Set in a rock ledge with unusual construction, and natural setting.

Safe House, Milwaukee, Wisconsin. **Why?** Spy theme restaurant. No sign and you need to know the password to get in.

Steam Plant, Spokane, Washington **Why?** One of the few historically renovated steam plants in the US.

Terry Bison Ranch, Cheyenne, Wyoming. **Why?** Go back in time to eat and drink up close and personal with bison.

Tonga Room, San Francisco, California **Why?** Experience tropical rain, thunder and lightning storms while you eat in the nostalgic Tonga Room and drink in the Hurricane Bar.

T-Rex Café, Lake Buena Vista, Florida. Family restaurant with, wait for it…life-sized animatronic dinosaurs, simulated meteor showers, and a bar with moving tentacles.

TWA Hotel, JFK Airport, New York. A real TWA Constellation and TWA flight center allows you to step back in time to 1962. Complete with roller skating rink

The Yurt at Solitude, Solitude, Utah. **Why?** After a guided snowshoe tour through a forest, you'll eat a five-course dinner in a Mongolian yurt.

Cambodia

Vista Bar and Restaurant, Song Saa, Koh Rong Archipelago, Sihanoukville. **Why?** Spectacular views on a private island, just a little bit over the top.

Canada

The 5 Fishermen, Halifax. **Why?** The restaurant was originally a funeral home that helped with the victims of the 1912 Titanic and 1917 Halifax explosion. Paranormal activity anyone?

O.Noir, Toronto and Montreal. **Why?** Dine in total darkness.

Signs, Toronto. **Why?** Dedicated to the deaf, but open for anyone.

Sultan's Tent and Café Moroc, Toronto. **Why?** A French Moroccan 3-course dinner lantern-lit tents on pillows. With belly dancing. In Canada. Perfect.

Czech Republic

Chodovar Brewery and Spa, Chodova Plana, Czech Republic. **Why?** The spa has, of course, a beer bath.

Dubai, UAE

Chill Out. Why? OK, this is weird. An Ice lounge in the Middle East. You can get hot food, hot drinks, and desserts in sub-zero temperature with changing lighting.

England

The Attendant, Fitzrovia, London. **Why?** It started life as a Victorian Toilet around 1890 and was brought back to life recently as a hip coffee shop and bakery.

Fiji

Namale Fiji, Savusavu. **Why?** Dine with ocean views, next to a waterfall, or in a candlelit sea cave on the beach.

Finland

Lapland Hotels SnowVillage, Kittilä. **Why?** 3 restaurants with two of them made with snow and ice.

Snowman World Ice Bar, Rovaniemi, Finland. **Why?** Opens December 6 through March 17. Located on the Artic Circle inside Santa Claus Village, everything is made of ice: glasses, chairs, tables.

France

Le Refuge des Fondus, Montmartre, Paris. **Why?** Eating fondue in a funky small café and drinking wine with feeding bottles (baby bottles complete with nipples) is just too good.

Sur un Arbre Perché, Paris. **Why?** Where else can you eat in a tree house with swing chairs and get a shiatsu massage!

Hungary

Ruin Bars, Budapest. Why? There are many "ruin bars" in Budapest. These are in previously unused, run down, derelict buildings that have been made into very hip, very lively, very fun bars. Szimpla Kert is one of the better known.

Iceland

Quest Hair, Beer and Whiskey Saloon, Reykjavik. **Why?** Because you can get a haircut and a drink, that's why.

Italy

Fortezza Medicea Restaurant, Siena. **Why?** Customers must pass a background check and several checkpoints, and all cutlery is plastic. It is housed in the town's Renaissance-era fortress, built 1474. It is a high-security prison for criminals serving no less than seven years.

Japan

Cannibalistic Sushi, Tokyo. **Why?** Sushi is hidden inside a realistic body and the waiter dissects the body to get the sushi. The packaging of the dishes is made of dough, and the special sauce imitates blood. All the sushi and sashimi have the forms of human organs. Yum.

Maid Cafes, Tokyo. **Why?** Enter into a fantasy world with waitresses dressed in maid costumes act as your servants and treat customers as masters and mistresses in a private home.

Niagara, Meguro-ku, Tokyo. **Why?** Each dish and drink is delivered by train that stops right in front of you.

Ninja Tokyo, Tokyo. **Why?** Enjoy ninja magic done by professional magicians.

Zauo, Shinjuku-ku, Tokyo. **Why?** You dine in a wooden boat in the middle of a large seafood tank where you will get a fishing pole, catch your seafood, and let your server know how you want it prepared.

Kenya

Ali Barbour's Cave Restaurant, Diani Beach. **Why?** Set inside an ancient coral cove and lit by candlelight.

Maldives

Ithaa Undersea Restaurant, Rangali Island. **Why?** Diners are 5 meters below the sea with clear panoramic views above and around.

Huvafen Fushi, North Male. **Why?** Taken by speedboat from the airport. Incredibly posh, choice of dining at 3 restaurants.

Netherlands

De Kas, Amsterdam. **Why?** Meals are served in an old greenhouse converted into a restaurant and nursery. The vegies, herbs, and edible flowers are grown right there.

Kinderkookkafe, Amsterdam. **Why?** Kids ages 8-12 years old sets the tables, cook and serve the meals to their own parents (with a little help from adults).

Philippines

The Labassin Waterfall Restaurant, Villa Escudero Resort, San Pablo City. **Why?** Diners are sitting in the water at the foot of the waterfall. Eat with your fingers and definitely no socks.

Villa Escudero, San Pablo. **Why?** Dine in a working coconut plantation.

Spain

El Diablo, Lanzarote. **Why?** The grill is on top of an opening to a volcano, where just 6 feet under lava is at 752 degrees.

Taiwan

Modern Toilet, Taipei City. **Why?** You know what the seats look like, and the meals are served in…wait for it…toilet bowl shaped dishes. What's not to like, besides, well, everything.

Thailand

Bird's Nest Restaurant, Soneva Kiri Eco Resort. **Why?** Diners are actually in a tree, up 16 feet with a great view. Your server uses a zip line to deliver food and drinks.

Cabbages and Condoms. Bangkok & other locations (also, in England and Japan). **Why?**

Hajime Robot Restaurant, Bangkok. **Why?** Robots deliver your food, takes your dirty plates, and dances when it has a moment.

Vertigo Restaurant and Moon Bar, Banyan Tree Hotel. Bangkok. **Why?** The Sky Bar appears to float above the city with incredible views of Bangkok.

UK

26 Grains Porridge Café, London, UK. **Why?** It's all about the porridge!

Zambia

Tongabezi Lodge, Livingstone. **Why?** Dine in a floating sampan

Zanzibar

The Rock Restaurant. Why? Located in a limestone cave that opens right on the beach.

In 61 Countries

Dinner in the Sky, 61 countries. **Why?** A crane lifts guests 160 feet in the air while strapped into dining chairs with duh! great views.

Chapter IV

HIGHLY
OPINIONATED

BOOKS, TV, MOVIES, MUSIC, AND MEDIA, OH MY!

Favorite Books About Restaurants

Behind the Kitchen Door by Saru Jayaraman (2014)

Fast Food Nation by Eric Schlosser (2001)

Good Things to Eat, As Suggested by Rufus: A Collection of Practical Recipes for Preparing Meats, Game, Fowl, Fish, Puddings, Pastries, Etc (1911, republished in 1999)

Grinding it out: The Making of McDonald's by Ray Kroc (2016)

The Hotel Keepers, Head Waiters, and Housekeepers' Guide by Tunis Campbell (1848)

How Starbucks Saved My Life by Michael Gill (2007)

Kitchen Confidential: Adventures in the Culinary Underbelly by Anthony Bourdain (2007)

Le Guide Culinaire by August Escoffier (1903)

The New Restaurant Manager, Parts 1 and 2 by John Self (Shameless, I know, but there it is) (2021)

Setting the Table: The Transforming Power of Hospitality in Business by Danny Meyer (2009)

Unreasonable Hospitality by Will Guidara (2022)

Movies About or Set in Restaurants
5 Favorite movies

Eat, Drink, Man, Woman (1994) – Wonderful film, funny and moving, with lots of food and restaurants. Comedy/Drama. A great chef has lost his sense of taste. His 3 grown daughters both help and complicate his life

The Big Night (1996) – There's a moral for restaurant owners: Give the customer what the customer wants, not what you want the customer to want

The Hundred Foot Journey (2014) Comedy/Drama. A family opens an Indian restaurant in France across the street from a Michelin star French restaurant

Estomago: A Gastronomic Story (2007) Brazilian comedy, drama. Unusual movie about someone who first cooks to survive, but later to win.

Chef (2014) Comedy/drama. A head chef quits his job to open a food truck
A Mi Me Gusta (2008) Comedy, romance
Alice's Restaurant (1969) Comedy, drama
**Babette's Feast* (1987) Drama
The Baker's Wife (1938) Comedy, drama
The Big Restaurant (1966) French comedy, thriller See Le Grande Restaurant below
Boiling Point (2021) Thriller, drama
Bon Appetit (2010). Comedy, Drama
Burnt (2015) Comedy, drama
Chef (2014) Adventure, comedy, drama

Highly Opinionated

The Chef (2012) Comedy, drama.
Cheeni Kum (2007) Comey, Drama, romance
Chocolat (2000) Drama, romance
Cloudy With Chance of Meatballs (2009) Animation, adventure, comedy
Cocktail (1988) Comedy, drama, romance
The Cook, The Thief, His Wife, & Her Lover (1989), Crime, romance.
Delicatessen (1991) Comedy, crime, strange
Dim Sum (2018, 2020) Comedy
Diner (1982, 2019) Comedy, drama
Dinner Rush (2000) Crime, Drama, Romance
Eat Pray Love (2010) Bio, drama, romance
Eating Raoul (1982) Comedy, crime
East Side Sushi (2014) Drama
The God of Cookery (1996) Action, comedy
Dinner Rush (2001) Crime, drama, romance
East Side Sushi (2014) Drama
Fried Green Tomatoes (1991) Comedy
Haute Cuisine (2012) Comedy, Bio
I am Love (2009) Drama
I Carry You With Me (2021) Drama
Hunger Games (2012) Ok, this is a stretch, but the title, the title…
Julie & Julia (2009) Bio, drama
Kitchen. The Last Battle (2017) Comedy
Kukhnya v Parizhe (2014) Comedy, romance
La Grande Bouffe (1973) Comedy, drama
Le Grand Restaurant (1966) Also known as What's Cooking in Paris. French comedy thriller
Le Chef (2012, US 2014) French comedy
Like Water for Chocolate (1992) Drama, romance
Love's Kitchen (2011) comedy, drama, romance
The Lunchbox (2013) Drama, romance
Mediterranean Food (2009) Comedy, romance
Midnight Diner (2014, 2019) Comedy/Drama
Midnight Diner 2 (2016) Drama
Mostly Martha (2001) Comedy, romance, drama
My Big Fat Greek Wedding (2002) Comedy
My Big Fat Greek Wedding 2 (2016) Comedy

My Dinner with Andre (1981) Comedy, drama
Mystic Pizza (1988) Comedy, drama
Nina's Heavenly Delights (2006) Comedy
No Reservations (2007) Comedy, drama, romance
Ratatouille (2007). Animated, comedy, adventure
Recipe for Love (2014) Comedy, romance
Restaurant (1998, 2006) Romantic comedy
Romantics Anonymous (2010) Comedy/Romance
Secret of the Grain (2007) Drama
Sideways (2004) Comedy, drama
Simply Irresistible (1999) Comedy, drama
The Slammin' Salmon (2009) Comedy
Soul Food (1997) Comedy, drama
Soul Kitchen (2009) Comedy, drama
Still Waiting (2009) Comedy
A Tale of Samurai Cooking: A True Love Story (2013) Drama, history
Tampopo (1985) Comedy, drama
A Taste of Hunger (2021) Drama, romance
A Taste of Romance (2012) comedy, drama
Tasting Menu (2013) Comedy
Today's Special (2009) Comedy
Tortilla Soup (2001) (Remake of Eat, Drink, Man, Woman) Comedy, romance, drama
The Trip (2010) Comedy, drama
Udon (2006) Comedy/Drama
Uncorked (2020) Drama
Vatel (2000) Bio, drama, Romance
Waiting (2005) Comedy
Waitress (2007) Comedy, drama, romance
Who is Killing the Great Chefs of Europe? (1978) Dark comedy, mystery
The Wing or the Thigh (1976) French comedy
Woman on Top (2000) Comedy, romance

** Academy Award winner or nominee

Favorite 6 Documentary Films

42 Grams (2017) Tough movie about what it takes to create a Michelin starred restaurant

Ella Brannan: Commanding the Table (2016). In depth portrait of the lady who was over a restaurant dynasty, including Commander's Palace in New Orleans for 50 years

Jiro Dreams of Sushi (2011) About Jiro Ono, a sushi master, his Tokyo restaurant, and his son

Love, Charlie: The Rise and Fall of Chef Charlie Trotter (2021) Brutal, intimate look at Charlie Trotter (1959-2013)

Somm (2012) The journey of four sommeliers hoping to pass the Master Sommelier exam

Spinning Plates (2012) About three very different restaurants and their owners

Documentaries/Reality TV

Andre & His Olive Tree (2020)
Avec Eric (2009 – 2015)
Barbecue (2018)
Bon Appetit with Gerard Depardieu (TV series 2015)
El Bulli: Cooking in Progress (2010)
Breakfast, lunch, and Dinner (2019)
Ella Brennan: Commanding the Table (2016)
Chef's Table (2015-2019)
Chef's Table: France (2016)
Constructing Albert (2017)
Cooked (2015-)
Fast Food Nation (2006)
Fed Up (2014)
Finding Gaston (2014)
Food Inc (2008)
For Grace (2015)
The Founder (2016)

The Restaurant Compendium for the Curious

The Inn at Little Washington: A Delicious New Documentary (2020)
Jeremiah Tower: The Last Magnificent (2016)
Kings of Pastry (2009)
The Last Supper: The Life of the Deathrow Chef (2005)
A Matter of Taste: Serving up Paul Liebrandt (2011)
Michelin Stars – Tales from the Kitchen (2017)
Noma: My Perfect Storm (2015)
Ottolenghi and the Cakes of Versailles (2020)
The Restaurateur (2010)
Roadrunner: A Film about Anthony Bourdain (2021)
Salt, fat, acid, heat (2018)
The Search for General Tso (2014)
Sour Grapes (2016)
Step Up to the Plate (2019)
Super-Size Me (2004)
A Tale of Two Kitchens (2019)
The Trip to Italy (2014)
What the Health (2017)

TV Series About Restaurants

2 Broke Girls (2011–2017)
Anthony Bourdain: No Reservations (2005-2012)
Anthony Bourdain: Parts Unknown (2013)
The Bear (2022-)
The Best Thing I Ever Ate (2009-)
Bob's Burgers (2011 -)
El Bulli (2010)
Cheers (1982–1993)
Chefs (2015-) 7.1
A Chef's Life (2013–2018)
The Chef Show (2019-)
Chef Wanted with Annie Burrell (2012-)
Chopped (2007-)
Chef's Table (2015-2019)
Diners, Drive-ins and Dives (2006 -)
Cutthroat Kitchen (2013–2017)
Diners, Drive-ins, and Dives (2007-)

The Event (2021)
Feed the Beast (2016) Crime, drama.
For the Love of Kitchens (2021)
Foundations of Cookery (1938)
Gordon Ramsay's 24 hours to Hell and Back (2018-)
Grand Maison Tokyo (2019-)
Hell's Kitchen (2005-)
In Search of Perfection (2006-2007)
Jamie's Kitchen (2002)
Joe's Kitchen (2020)
Kimchi Family (2011-2012)
The Kitchen (2012-2016) Adventure, comedy, drama.
Kitchen Confidential (2005-2006) Comedy, romance.
Kitchen Nightmares (2007-2014)
Kitchen Casino (2014)
Kukhnya v Parizhe (2014)
Love at First Bite (2018)
Man Finds Food (2015-)
Man v. Food (2008-)
Mexico – One Plate at a Time (2003–2019)
Midnight Diner (2009)
Midnight Diner (2016)
Million Pound Menu (2018–2019)
Mind of a Chef (2012-)
Mystery Diners (2011)
Opening Night (2019)
The Restaurant (2003, 2017)
Restaurant Stakeout (2012-)
Restaurant Startup (2014-2016)
Restaurant Impossible (2011-)
Restaurants on the Edge (2019)
Road Tasted (2006)
Road Tasted with the Neelys (2008)
Somebody Feed Phil (2018–)
Step up to the Plate (2019)
Sweetbitter (2018-2019)
Sweet Munchies (2020)
The Bear (2022-)

Toast (2010)
Ugly Delicious (2018-)
Undercover Chef (2020-)
Unique Eats (2011-)
Vanderpump Rules (2013-)
Wahlburgers (2014-2019)
Welcome to Sweetie Pie's (2011-)
Whites (2010)
Wok of Love (2018)

Advertising Campaigns That Needed Do-Overs

McDonald's "When the US wins, you win." (1984). During the 1984 Olympics, McDonald's gave out scratcher cards with every McDonald's purchase. If the US won a gold medal, you'd get a free Big Mac. Sounds great, but for one little thing. The Soviet Union, East Germany, and North Korea did not compete in the Olympics meaning that the US won many, *many* more gold medals than expected. The New York Times called the number of Big Macs given away as "mindboggling."

Burger King "Where's Herb" (1986). The ad lasted all of three months. Herb was someone who had never eaten at Burger King and the public was asked to identify Herb in a Burger King. Burger King spent millions on the ad campaign, but the public showed little interest in finding Herb. Burger King changed ad agencies after this, and some say "Herb" was one of the worst ad campaigns in history.

Domino's "The Noid" (1986). It was meant to be a play on the word annoyed. The Noid was a Claymation man with rabbit ears whose purpose was to stop the delivery of fresh pizzas, but Domino's could stop the noid. This was a successful campaign until a 22-year-old man, Kenneth Lamar Noid, believed the character was based on him. In 1989, he held two Domino's employee's hostage at gunpoint. The hostages escaped, and Noid was caught. He spent time in a mental institution and committed suicide in 1995.

McDonald's McAfrika (2002). Hamburger sold in Norway and Denmark. Supposedly based on an African recipe. The problem was the timing. When it was released, several countries in Africa were facing starvation. The ad campaign was relaunched in 2008 and faced the same criticism.

Red Lobster, "Endless Crab" (2003). Customers could order as many plates of snow crab as they wanted for a set price. Red Lobster would make a profit when customers ate one or two plates but would lose money with the third plate. Most customers ate more than three plates, the ad campaign happened when wholesale snow crab prices were high (and went higher), and the final problem was that snow crab takes a long time to eat and customers stayed much longer in the restaurants.

Quiznos' Spongemonkeys (2004). Fairly bizarre ad that had creatures singing "We love the subs." The commercial caused more attention to the creatures than to Quiznos.

Carl's Jr.'s and Hardee's (2005). Media called Carl's Jr.'s "Slutburger" campaign started with Paris Hilton sexily eating a burger.

Burger King, "Whopper Virgins" (2008). Burger King traveled to remote areas of the world to find burger "virgins" to comparison taste test Whoppers and Big Macs in countries like Transylvania and Greenland. The ad offended many because of the poverty in many of the areas.

McDonald's hashtag, #McDStories (2012) McDonald's thought they would get nice stories about their food, but instead got stories that bashed the company (bashtags). The campaign made it on several "worst" lists for social media blunders.

Arby's 1-855-MEAT-HLP (2015). Made fun of vegetarians who did not see the joke.

McDonald's "Pay with Lovin'" (2015) Ran from February 2 and ended on Valentine's Day in 2015. Customers in McDonald's would be randomly chosen and could pay for their meal by showing love to a family member, like calling their sister, hugging their mother, or uh, dancing. McDonald's gave away more than a million free meals without much of a surge in sales.

Some of the Best Advertising Campaigns

1924 **"Less Work for Mother."** Horn and Hardart opened automats that had prepackaged foods behind windows for take-out meals.

1970's **"You Deserve a Break Today."** McDonald's. According to Ad Age, it is the top-rated advertising jingle of all time. This was McDonald's first national TV ad campaign and lasted for 43 years.

1980's **"Burger Wars"**. Burger King was the first to place an attack ad.

1984 **"Where's the Beef?"** Wendy's. The ad was actually titled "Fluffy Bun" and starred actress Clara Peller. The ad was super successful as it boosted Wendy's revenue by 31% that year.

1991 **"Have it Your Way,"** Burger King. Customers could choose various toppings.

1993 **"Nothing but Net,"** McDonald's. Superbowl ad 'The Showdown' with Michael Jordan and Larry Bird.

Current **Pal's Sudden Service,** homey, quirky, over-the-top, too cutesy, and way too wholesome, but there's just something about the ads that make you smile.

Restaurant Ad Campaigns with Mixed Results

Domino's "30 minutes or it's free." 1979- 1980's. In 1979, Domino's started the "30 minutes or free pizza" campaign, guaranteeing customers would get their pizza free if they didn't get their order within 30 minutes of placing their order.

The 30-minute delivery guarantee drove amazing growth with Dominos growing from 200 stores in 1978, then to 5,000 by 1989. The guarantee was successful in helping Domino's to be known as the fast delivery company.

But, in order to deliver pizzas on time, delivery drivers drove recklessly and caused dozens of accidents, with over 20 fatalities in the 1980s. In 1998, Tom Monaghan sold his stake in Domino's for $1 billion.

Starbucks "Race Together." 2015. The racial climate in late 2014 was tense when the white police officer was not indicted for the shooting death of an 18-year-old African American male. The CEO of Starbucks, Howard Schultz started the ad campaign that instructed the baristas to write "#racetogether" on every cup served and, if the barista wanted to, to engage with customers about race relations.

Songs About Food and Restaurants

"Alice's Restaurant" by Arlo Guthrie
"American Fast Food" by Randy Stonehill
"American Pie" by Don McLean
"Breakfast in America" by Supertramp
"Carmalita" by Warren Zevon Sunset Grille by Don Henley
"Cheeseburger in Paradise" by Jimmy Buffett
"Compliments of Your Waitress" by Chumbawamba
"The Continuing Decline of Customer Service" by My God, The Heat
    "Copacabana" by Barry Manilow
"Sad I" by The Eagles
"D's Diner" by Les Claypool
"Diner" by Widespread Panic
"The Diner Song" by State Radio
"Down at the Twist and Shout" by Mary Chapin-Carpenter
"Drive Thru" by Leslie Deep
"Drive-Thru" by Tenacious D
"Drive Thru" by Young Chozen
"The Drive Thru" by Jake Miller
"Escape (The Pina Colada Song)" by Rupert Holmes
"Fast Food Service" by Plasmatics
"Fast Food" by Kidsongs
"Fast Food Messiahs" by Junesex
"The Fast-Food Song" by Fast Food Rockers
"Fast Food" by Richard Thompson
"Food For the Earth" by SkeletonDealer
"Food Service Establishment" by Bubbles
"Food Song" by Buck 65

The Restaurant Compendium for the Curious

"Granny Diner" by Grizzly Bear
"Hip Hop Food Order" by Lazee Lamont
"Fast Food Messiahs" by Junesex
"Food Service Manager" by Lazee Lamont
"Food Services" by Stardice
"Ice Cream Man" by Van Halen
"Ihop" by Luna
"Kim The Waitress" by Material Issue
"Junk Food Junkie" by Larry Groce
"Late Night Diner" by Adam Hood
"Magic Chicken" by Aquabats
"Mary's Place" by Bruce Springsteen
"Melrose Diner" by Richard Elliot
"Nickel and Dimed" from American Ruling Class Soundtrack
"Open All Night" by Bruce Springsteen
"The Prettiest Waitress in Memphis" by Cory Branan
"Recipe" by G. Love & Special Sauce
"Sad Café" by The Eagles
"Satan Gave Me a Taco" by Beck The Slant/The Diner by Ani DiFranco
"Scenes From an Italian Restaurant" by Billy Joel
"Soul Kitchen" by The Doors
"The Slant/The Diner" by Ani DiFranco
"Sunset Grille" by Don Henley
"Top Hat Bar and Grille" by Jim Croce
"Tom's Diner" by Suzanne Vega
"Trapped In the Drive-Thru" by "Weird Al" Yankovic
"Waitress In The Sky" by The Replacements
"What Do You Want" by Parker Paul

Bands and Singers With Food Names

Ambrosia
The Black-Eyed Peas
Blind Melon
Blue Oyster Cult
Bowling for Soup
Bread
Cake
Chuck Berry

The Cranberries
Cream
Fiona Apple
The Flying Burrito Brothers
Hall and Oates
Humble Pie
Jellyroll
Korn
Limp Bizkit
Marshmello
Meatloaf (RIP)
Peaches and Herb
Pearl Jam
Phish
The Raspberries
Red Hot Chili Peppers
Salt-N-Pepa
Smashing Pumpkins
Spice Girls
Strawberry Alarm Clock
Taco
Vanilla Fudge
Vanilla Ice

Songs With Food in the Title

"American Honey" by Lady Antebellum
"American Pie" by Don McLean
"Bacon" by Nick Jonas
"Banana Pancakes" by Jack Johnson
"Biscuits" by Kacey Musgraves
"Blueberry Hill" by Fats Domino
"Bread and Butter" by The Newbeats
"Brown Sugar" by The Rolling Stones
"Buttered Popcorn" by The Supremes
"Cake" by Melanie Martin
"Cake" by the Ocean by DNCE
"Cheeseburger in Paradise" by Jimmy Buffett Cherry Pie by Warrant
"Cherry Bomb" by John Cougar Mellencamp

"Cherry Pie" by Sade
"Cherry on Top" by Jake Owen
"Chicken Fried" by Zac Brown Band Collard Greens and Cornbread by Fantasia
"Chicken and Biscuits" by Colt Ford
"Cold Budweiser and a Sweet Potatoe" by Joe Diffie
"Corn Fed" by Shannon Brown
"Corn Star" by Craig Morgan
"Cornflake Girl" by Tori Amos
"Corned Beef City" by Mark Knopfler
"Do Fries Go With That Shake?" By George Clinton
"Do You Want Fries With That" by Tim McGraw
"Fried Neckbones and Some Home Fries" by Santana
"Fruitcakes" by Jimmy Buffett
"Georgia Peaches", by Lauren Alaina
"Glass Onion" by The Beatles
"Good Brown Gravy" by Joe Diffie
"Gravy (For My Mashed Potatoes)" by Dee Dee Sharp
"Green Bananas" by Jake Owen
"Grits Ain't Groceries" by Little Milton
"Honey Bee" by Blake Shelton
"Hot Potato" by The Kinks
"I Can't Help Myself" (Sugar Pie, Honey Bunch) by Four Tops
"Ice Cream Man" by Van Halen
"Ice Cream" by Sarah MacLaclan
"I Got Green Beans, Potatoes, Tomatoes" by Shirley Caesar
"I've Got a Lovely Bunch of Coconuts" by Danny Kaye
"I Heard it Through the Grapevine" by Marvin Gaye
"I Still Like Bologna" by Alan Jackson
"Jambalaya (on the Bayou)" by The Carpenters
"Key Lime Pie" by Kenny Chesney
"Lady Marmalade" by Christina Aguilera, Labelle, Lil' Kim, Mya, Pink
"Lemon" by U2
"The Lemon Song" by Led Zeppelin
"Lollipop" by The Chordettes
"Mashed Potato Time" by Dee Dee Sharp
"Meat and Potatoes Man" by Alan Jackson
"Milkshake and Potato Chips" by Bob Marley

Highly Opinionated

"Milkshake" by Kelis
"Milkshake" by The Village People
"Nicotine and Gravy" by Beck
"Old Dogs, Children, and Watermelon Wine" by Tom T. Hall
"Peaches" by the Presidents of the United States
"Peanut Butter Jelly" by Galanti8s
"Peanut Butter Jelly Time" by Buckwheat Boyz
"Pizza Day" by The Aquabats
"Pizza Girl" by Jonas Brothers
"Pizza Pie" by Systems of a Down
"Polk Salad Annie" by Elvis Presley
"Pork and Beans" by Weezer
"Pour Some Sugar On Me" by Def Leppard
"Put the Lime in the Coconut" by Harry Nilsson
"Raspberry Beret" by Prince
"Rock Lobster" by The B-52's
"Rub Some Bacon on It" by Rhett & Link
"Sandwich and a Soda" by Tamia
"Strawberry Fields Forever by the Beatles
"Strawberry Swing" by Coldplay
"Sweet Pea" by Tommy Roe
"Strawberry Wine" by Deana Carter
"Sweet Potato Pie" by James Taylor
"Taco Tuesday" by Lil John
"Tangerine" by Led Zeppelin
"Tangerine Dreams" by Charlie Puth
"Watermelon Crawl" by Tracy Byrd
"Watermelon Sugar" by Harry Styles
"Where Corn Don't Grow" by Travis Tritt

LET'S EAT!

Slow it down with 'Slow Food'

"Slow Food" is a global, grassroots organization, founded in 1989 to prevent the disappearance of local food cultures and traditions, counteract the rise of fast life and combat people's dwindling interest in the food they eat, where it comes from, and how our food choices affect the world around us. (slowfood.com)

James Beard Outstanding Restaurant Awards
THE JAMES BEARD FOUNDATION

1991 Bouley, New York, New York (closed in 2017)
1992 Chez Panisse, Berkeley, California
1993 The Inn at Little Washington, Washington, Virginia
1994 Spago, West Hollywood, California
1995 Le Cirque, New York, New York (closed 2018)
1996 Commander's Palace, New Orleans, Louisiana
1997 Union Square Café, New York, New York
1998 Le Bernardin, New York, New York
1999 The Four Seasons, New York, New York (closed 2020)
2000 Charlie Trotter's, Chicago, Illinois
2001 Campanile, Los Angeles, California
2002 Gotham Bar and Grill, New York, New York
2003 Zuni Cafe, San Francisco, California
2004 Chanterelle, New York, New York (closed 2009)
2005 Galatoire's, New Orleans, Louisiana
2006 The French Laundry, Yountville, California
2007 Frontera Grill, Chicago, Illinois
2008 Gramercy Tavern, New York, New York
2009 Jean-Georges, New York, New York

Highly Opinionated

2010 Daniel, New York, New York
2011 Eleven Madison Park, New York, New York
2012 Boulevard, San Francisco, California
2013 Blue Hill Restaurant, New York, New York
2014 The Slanted Door, San Francisco, California
2015 Blue Hill at Stone Barns, Tarrytown, New York
2016 Alinea, Chicago, Illinois
2017 Topolobampo, Chicago, Illinois
2018 Highlands Bar and Grill, Birmingham, Alabama
2019 Zahav, Philadelphia, Pennsylvania
2020 Canceled due to COVID-19
2021 Canceled due to COVID-19
2022 Chai Pani, Ashville, North Carolina

The World's Most Luxurious Restaurants
guide.michelin.com (9 July, 2021)

China

Taian Table, Shanghai

France

France Alléno Paris au Pavillon Ledoyen, Paris
Le Cinq, Paris

Germany

Vendôme, Bergisch Gladbac (near Cologne)

Macau

Alain Ducasse at Morpheus, Macau

Monaco

Le Louis XV, in the Alain Ducasse a l'Hôtel de Paris, Monte-Carlo

Singapore

Zen, Outram

South Korea

Gaon, Seoul

Switzerland

Restaurant de l'Hôtel de Ville, Crissier (near Lausanne)

Taiwan

A Cut, Taipei

Thailand

Le Normandie, Bangkok

USA

Jungsik, New York
The Inn at Little Washington, DC

HIGHLY OPINIONATED

The Best Restaurants According to 'La Liste' and 'The World's Best 50 Restaurants'
La Liste, The World's Best Restaurant Selection

Based on the compilation of hundreds of guidebooks, thousands of media publications, and millions of online reviews, LA LISTE offers the world's best restaurant selection at your fingertips wherever you go.

99.50 Guy Savoy, Paris, France
99.00 L'Arpège, Paris, France
99.00 L'Auberge du Vieux Puits, Fontjoncouse, France
99.00 La Vague d'Or – Le Cheval Blanc, Saint-Tropez, France
99.00 Martin Berasategui, Lasarte-Oria, Spain
99.00 Schwarzwaldstube, Baiersbronn, Germany
99.00 Frantzén, Stockholm, Sweden
99.00 Le Bernardin, New York, USA
99.00 Restaurant de l'Hôtel de Ville, Crissier, Switzerland
98.50 L'Assiette Champenoise, Tinqueux, France
98.50 Da Vittorio, Brusaporto, Italy
98.50 Le Louis XV-Alain Ducasse, Monaco, Monaco
98.50 Le Calandre, Sarmeola de Rubano, Italy
98.50 Sushi Saito, Minato-ku, Japan
98.00 L'Ambroisie, Paris, France
98.00 L'Oustaùde Baumanière, Les Baux-de-Prevence, France
98.00 Régis et Jacques Marcon, Saint-Bonnet-le-Froid, France
98.00 Aqua, Wolfsburg, Germany
98.00 Cheval Blanc by Peter Knogl, Basel, Switzerland
98.00 Core by Clare Smyth, London, UK
97.50 Pavillon Ledoyen, Paris, France
97.50 Mirazur, Menton, France
97.50 Troisgros-Le Bois sans Fruilles, Ouches, France
97.50 Maison Pic, Valence, France
97.50 Victor's Fine Dining by Christian Bau, Perl, Germany
97.50 Don Alfonso 1890, Massa Lubrense, Italy
97.50 Oteria Francescana, Modena, Italy
97.50 Dal Pescatore, Runate, Italy

The Restaurant Compendium for the Curious

97.50 Atelier Crenn, San Francisco, USA
97.50 Inter Scaldes, Kruiningen, Netherlands
97.50 Zilte, Antwerp, Belgium
97.50 Schloss Schauenstein, Furstenau, Switzerland
97.50 The French Laundry, Yountville, USA
97.50 Yanagiya, Mizunami-shi, Japan
97.00 Pierre Gagnaire, Paris, France
97.00 Le Pre Catelan, Paris, France
97.00 Les Pres d'Eugenie-Michel Guerard
97.00 El Celler de Can Roca, Girona, Spain
97.00 Vendome, Bergisch Gladbach, Germany
97.00 La Trota, Rivodutri, Italy
97.00 Manresa, Los Gatos, USA   41
97.00 Georges Blanc, Vonnas, France
97.00 Obauer, Werfen, Austria
97.00 Waldhotel Sonnora, Dreis, Germany
97.00 Matsukawa, Minato-ku, Japan
97.00 "The Capital" at the Beijin, Bejing, China
97.00 Single Thread, Healdsburg, USA
97.00 Zen, Singapore, Singapore
96.50 Arzak, Donostia, Spain
96.50 Vila Joya, Albufeira, Portugal

The World's 50 Best Restaurants in the World

Started in 2002, 'The World's 50 Best Restaurants in the World' uses a panel of 1,080 culinary experts and has structured and audited voting procedure.

1. Geranium, Copenhagen, Denmark
2. Central, Lima, Peru
3. Disfrutar, Barcelona, Spain
4. Diverxo, Madrid, Spain
5. Pujol, Mexico City, Mexico Odette, Singapore
6. Asador Etxebarri, Atxondo, Spain
7. A Casa do Porco, Sao Paulo, Brazil
8. Lido 84, Gardone Riviera, Italy
9. Quintonil, Mexico City, Mexico
10. Le Calandre, Rubano, Italy

11. Maido, Lima, Peru
12. Uliassi, Senigallia, Italy
13. Steirereck, Vienna, Austria
14. Don Julio, Buenos Aires, Argentina
15. Reale, Castel di Sangro, Italy
16. Elkano, Getaria, Spain
17. Nobelhart & Schmutzig, Berlin, Germany
18. Alchemist, Copenhagen, Denmark
19. Piazza Duomo, Alba, Italy
20. Den, Tokyo, Japan
21. Mugaritz, San Sebastian, Spain
22. Septime, Paris, France
23. The Jane, Antwerp, Belgium
24. The Chairman, Hong Kong
25. Frantzén, Stockholm, Sweden
26. Restaurant Tim Raue, Berlin, Germany
27. Hof Van Cleve, Kruishoutem, Belgium
28. Le Clarence, Paris, France
29. St. Hubertus, San Cassiano, Italy
30. Florilège, Tokyo, Japan
31. Arpège, Paris, France
32. Mayta, Lima, Peru
33. Atomix, New York, USA
34. Hisa Franko, Kobarid, Slovenia
35. The Clove Club, London, England
36. Odette, Singapore
37. Fyn, Cape Town, South Africa
38. Jordnaer, Copenhagen, Denmark
39. Sorn, Bangkok, Thailand
40. Schloss Schauenstein, Furstenau, Switzerland
41. La Cime, Osaka, Japan
42. Quique Dacosta, Denia, Spain
43. Boragó, Santiago, Chile
44. La Bernardin, New York, USA
45. Narisawa, Tokyo, Japan
46. Belcanto, Lisbon, Portugal
47. Oteque, Rio de Janeiro, Brazil
48. Leo, Bogotá, Columbia

49. Ikoyi, London, England
50. Single Thread, Healdsburg, USA

Michelin stars

A rating system used to grade restaurants on their quality. The guide was originally made in 1900 to show French drivers where local restaurants and mechanics were. The rating system was first introduced in 1926 with one star and in 1933, the second and third stars were added. According to the Guide, one star signifies "a very good restaurant," two stars are "excellent cooking that is worth a detour," and three stars mean "exceptional cuisine that is worth a special journey."

In 2003, some people blamed Michelin when French Chef Bernard Loiseau committed suicide amid rumors that his three Michelin star restaurant was about to lose a star. However, he was also suffering from depression because of debt and decreasing sales.

Luxe Digital's Top 11 Michelin Star Restaurants of 2021
(https://luxe.digital/)

Central, Lima, Peru (Best value)
Bon-Bon, Brussels, Belgium (Best in Belgium)
Atlier Crenn, San Francisco, USA (Best in California)
Le Bernardin, New York, USA (Best in New York)
Mirazur, Menton, France (Best in France)
The Fat Duck, Bray, UK (Best in UK)
Den, Tokyo, Japan (Best in Japan)
Noma, Copenhagen, Denmark (Best in Denmark)
Attica, Melbourne, Australia (Best in Australia)
Liao Fan Hong Kong, Singapore (Best budget)
Ultraviolet, Shanghai, China (Most expensive)

World's Most Expensive Michelin Restaurants (2022)
(ChefsPencil.com)

Sublimotion, Ibiza, Spain ($1,673 per person)

Highly Opinionated

Ultraviolet, Shanghai, China ($1,400 per person)
Masa, New York, USA ($950)
Kyoto Kitcho Arashiyama, Kyoto, Japan ($820 per person)
Ciel Bleu, Amsterdam, Netherlands ($664 per person)
Guy Savoy, Paris, France ($636)
Kikunoi Honten, Kyoto, Japan $582
Piazza Duomo, Alba, Italy $580
Alchemist, Copenhagen, Denmark $570
Forum, Hong Kong, $521
Gion Maruyama, Kyoto, Japan $519
The French Laundry, California, USA $500
Joel Robuchon, Tokyo, Japan $492
Shoukowa, Singapore, $480
Azabu Kadowaki, Tokyo, Japan $476

3 Ways to Score a Cheap(ish) Michelin Star Restaurant Meal

Go for lunch, order off the a-la-carte menu, or try one of the few Michelin starred street food vendors.

The 2021 Michelin Guide includes 132 restaurants with 3 Michelin stars

Countries with 3-star Michelin restaurants:

- France (including Monaco) 30
- Japan 22
- USA 13
- Italy 11
- Spain 11
- Germany 10
- Hong Kong and Macau 10
- United Kingdom 7
- Switzerland 3
- China 3
- Singapore 3

- Netherlands 2
- South Korea 2
- Belgium 2
- Denmark 2
- Austria 1
- Sweden 1
- Taiwan 1

Most Expensive Individual Restaurant Dishes

$25,000 Grand Velas Tacos: Frida Restaurant, Grand Velas Los Cabos Resort, Mexico

Langoustine, Kobe beef, Almas Beluga caviar, black truffle brie cheese, salsa with dried Morita chili peppers, Ley .925 anejo tequila, civet coffee, served on a gold flake-infused corn tortilla.

$23,000/2.2 lbs Beluga Almas Caviar, Beluga, Dubai, UAE

Almas translates to diamond and is the most expensive caviar in the world. It is very scarce as only about 22 pounds are harvested each year. It comes from albino beluga sturgeons (huso huso), which are between 60 - 100 years old and found only in the southern Caspian Sea. It is light colored, with plump and delicate orbs with a briny, creamy and buttery flavor. Naturally, it is sold in 24K gold tins.

$14,500 Fortress Stilt Fisherman Indulgence: Fortress Resort and Spa, Galle, Sri Lanka

Italian Cassata flavored with Baileys and served with pomegranate and mango compote. The base is champagne sabayon and 80-carat aquamarine stone, placed below a handcrafted chocolate stilt fisherman.

$12,000 Louis XIII Pizza, Salerno, Italy

Catered in your home with pizza chef, Renato Viola, sommelier, and chef. Dishes and cutlery are exclusive for this experience. Dough is direct mix 72-hour proofing, certified organic flour A.I.A.B, natural yeast, and Australian pink salt from the Murray River. Ingredients include 3 kinds of caviar: caviar Oscietra Royal Prestige, Kaspia Oscietra

Royal Classic caviar, and Beluga Caviar Kaspia; red Acciaroli Cilento prawns, lobster Palinurus elephas from Norway, Cicada in the Mediterranean (squilla mantis), and paired with Remy Martin Cognac Louis XIII and Krug Clos du Mesnil 1995 champagne with organic DOP buffalo mozzarella

$5 per kernel or $2, 500/6.5gallon tin Billion-dollar popcorn, Berco's Popcorn, Chicago, Illinois, USA

Organic sugar, butter from Vermont Creamery, Nielsen Massey Bourbon Vanilla, and Laeso salt, the most expensive salt in the world. Lastly, the caramel corn is covered in 23K edible gold flake.

$100 or $1,000 The zillion dollar lobster frittata: Norma's, Le Parker Meridien Hotel, Manhattan, New York

With 1oz of Sevruga caviar or 10 oz of Sevruga caviar

SERVICE TYPES

French Service
This is the most elaborate, labor intensive, expensive, and most formal of all the services.

French service usually requires two waiters, a front waiter and a back waiter, to serve. The front waiter prepares foods tableside, explains details about the food, and sometimes assists with wine pairings. The back waiter does the more unskilled tasks, like filling water glasses and clearing plates. Hot foods are cooked on a rechaud (hot plate) that sits on a gueridon (small table). Cold foods, such as salads, are assembled on the gueridon. Servers plate the finished foods onto individual plates and serve them to guests from right to left. (This is the only style of service where food is served from the right). Some foods, such as desserts, are displayed on a separate rolling dessert cart tableside, so the guests can choose their desserts of choice.

Russian Service (platter service)
Foods are cooked tableside with no courses placed on the table. Each course is served at the table. Servers put the foods on platters and then pass the platters. Guests help themselves to the foods and assemble their own plates.

English Service (butler service or family service)
Large serving platters and bowls are set on the dining tables in front of the guests by servers. Dishes are served at the table from the left using a serving spoon and fork and at times fish or carving knives. A waiter must be able to use only one hand to hold the spoon and fork while the other hand holds the dish.

American Service (plate service)
This is the least formal, requiring the least labor, and is the quickest.
Foods are pre-portioned in the kitchen, arranged on plates, with the salad and bread and butter the only exceptions, and served from the left with beverages served from the right. Used dishes and glasses are removed from the right. This is the most functional, common, economical, controllable, and efficient type of service.

Small Plates, Anyone?
Dim Sum (China), **Tapas** (Spain), **Meze** (Mediterranean), and **Banchan** (South Korea)

Setting the Table

I know you know this but…

Forks go on the left of the plate, even if you are left-handed. The knife is to the right of the plate, with the blade toward the plate, with the spoon on the outside.

For many courses, there are many forks. Forks are arranged according to the order of use, so the outside fork is for the appetizer, the middle fork is for the main dish, and the salad fork is on the inside. Silverware for fruit and dessert is always placed on top of the plate next to the glasses, which is also why this silverware is smaller.

Highly Opinionated

How to Spot the Dessert Fork

The dessert fork is usually a little smaller than the salad fork and is easily identified by looking at the left most tine. (Tines are the little prongs on the fork.) This left-most tine is a little larger than the others with a flattened edge allowing the user to hold a plate in the left hand and cut through the dessert with the left edge.

Lots of Forks!

Oyster forks	Table fork
Lobster forks	Toasting fork
Terrapin forks	Dessert fork
Pastry forks	Extendable fork
Fish forks	Granny fork
Fruit fork	Salad forks
Spaghetti fork	Berry forks
Dinner fork	Sardine forks
Cocktail fork	Pickle forks
Carving fork	Lettuce forks
Spork (apologies)	

Best Seats!

The best seats are inside the kitchen at the chef's table. They sometimes have bar type seating to save kitchen space and varies from 4 to a maximum of 8 seats. You'll have a great view of the hectic, crazy, yet highly orchestrated dance in the kitchen. Not every restaurant has these, but ask, they just might.

A sampling of restaurants with chef's tables

US

Alba, Des Moines, Iowa
Blood & Sand, St. Louis, Missouri
Boca, Cincinnati, Ohio

Buca di Beppo, multiple locations
Frasca Food & Wine, Boulder, Colorado
Gan Shan Station, Asheville, NC
Restaurant Guy Savoy, Caesar's Palace, Las Vegas, Nevada
Sea Salt, Naples, Florida
The Pearl, Nantucket, Massachusetts

International

Gaddi's, The Peninsula Hong Kong
Meurice Alain Ducasse, Paris, France
VEA, The Wellington, Hong Kong

We All Want to be a VIP

Restaurants and nightclubs try to anticipate everything that VIPs might want

VIP TABLE

- Raised, so can see what's happening
- All guests have equal seating
- Easy to get in and out for bathroom visits
- Soft booth seating preferable
- Placed in best room or best area of the restaurant
- Can see and be seen (VIPs do not want to be stared at. At least, not too much and only in a good way)

VIP GOOD PARTS:
Hosted entry
Personal server, so you never have to (gasp) stand in line
Best seats, best location

VIP BAD PARTS:
Better look the part (especially in nightclubs)
Mandatory minimum dollar spend

Organization of a Fine Dining Restaurant:

General Manager/COO: In charge of both kitchen (BOH/Back Of the House) and dining room (FOH/Front Of the House)

FOH (Front of House)
Dining room, bar, servers, hosts, bussers

Maitre d' (from maître d' hotel: French for "master of the house") Oversees the seating chart, VIP's, greets guests, and ensures servers and guests are seated efficiently.

Floor manager: Oversees entire dining room.

Captain: Usually found in very formal restaurants, but not all of them. The captain oversees several tables in a section along with the front and back waiters, runners, and bussers assigned to the section. Usually greets each table, takes drink and appetizer orders, and then the entrée, dessert, after dinner drinks, coffee orders, and presents the check. One of the most important duties is to pace each meal, making sure each course comes at the right time. The captain also handles table side service, like filleting fish or carving meat.

Front waiter: Greeting, order taking, service interactions with guests, handling the bill.

Back waiter/busser: Refills water glasses, clears dirty dishes, and 'crumbs' the table.

Server: When no front and back waiters, does everything that they do.

Sommelier: Recommends wine pairing with foods to the guests. Also creates wine menus and purchases the wine.

Runner: Brings prepared dishes from the kitchen to the table. Using the table positions (see illustration) the runner can place dishes in front of the correct guests.

BOH (Back of House)
Also called the heart of the house
The kitchen: chefs, cooks, dishwashers, prep

The hierarchy of a large restaurant kitchen includes five levels: executive chef, head chef/chef de cuisine, sous chef, chef de partie (a chef in charge of a particular station) and a commis chef (junior chef).

Executive Chef: Over multiple kitchen operations.

Chef de Cuisine (Head Chef): Oversees the menu, preparation, cooking, ordering, and the operations of the kitchen.

Chef de Partie: Chef in charge of a particular station.

Sous Chef: Just under the head chef. Helps supervise the kitchen.

Banquet Chef (Chef de Cuisines, catering chef): Oversees dining for large parties, events, and offsite locations.

Pastry Chef: Creates and makes all desserts.

Garde Manger (Pantry chef): In charge of all cold food items, like salads and meat and cheese trays.

Line Cook: Usually responsible for one menu item, like frying, grilling, etc.

Commis Chef (Prep cook): Usually a junior member of the kitchen staff who assists senior chefs with food preparation and organization. They can be assigned to one station, or they might float between different stations, as needed.

Expediter/Expo/Wheel man: Stands in front of the chefs, calls out and groups orders to the chefs. Similar to a conductor in an orchestra since the expo can have a tremendous influence on the efficiency of the kitchen.

Kitchen Steward/porter: Cleans, stocks, and organizes

Porter: Keeps the kitchen clean and neat

Dishwasher: Cleans all dishes, utensils, glasses, pots, and pans

How the server knows who gets what without asking

Servers, bussers, runners, and managers are all trained to stand at the same point of a table. The table has position numbers, usually starting to the right of the server, so that each customer can be identified. Servers stand at the same place each time, so no matter which customer goes first, the server knows who gets the correct menu item.

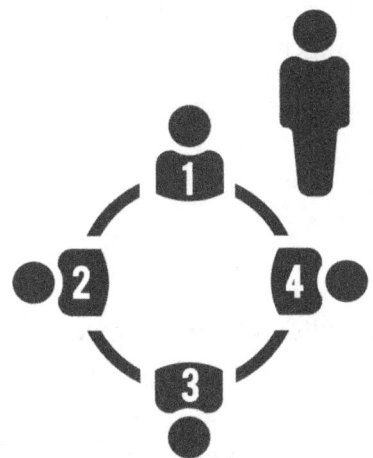

Restaurant Dinner Courses

In general, there are 12 courses, arriving in the following order:

1st **course**: Hors d'oeuvres

2nd **course**: Amuse bouche (pronounced ah-mooz boosh) - Small bite (much smaller than an appetizer) that is usually presented by the server as a gift from the chef or the kitchen and never included in the check. It is a finger food meant to get you ready for the main food.

3rd **course**: Soup

4th **course**: Appetizer

5th **course**: Salad

6th **course**: Fish

7th **course**: **First main dish** - Usually a white meat, such as turkey, chicken, or duck

8th **course**: **Palate cleanser** - Attempts to remove lingering tastes from your mouth so that you can enjoy the next course. Sorbet, prosecco, or water with lemon are commonly used.

9th **course**: **Second main dish** - Typically, a red meat, such as beef, lamb, or venison.

10th **course**: Cheese plate

11th **course**: **Dessert** - Usually accompanied by coffee, tea, dessert wine, or port.

12th **course**: **After dinner drinks and pastries** - Usually accompanied by coffee, tea, port, brandy, or scotch.

Chopsticks Etiquette

Chopsticks should only be used for picking up food, never to spear food and never, ever to point at people, pick teeth, bang, or move bowls, chewed on, or waved. They should be held so that the ends are even, and never held in each hand.

When not in use, chopsticks should be left on chopstick rests when provided, or placed across the bowl or plate.

Dining in China

In most traditional Chinese dining, dishes are shared on round tables with Lazy Susan turntables for easy sharing.

A basic place setting consists of a small teacup; a large plate with a small, empty rice bowl; a set of chopsticks usually on the right of the plate; and a soup spoon. Additions may include a chopstick rest or holder, a large water or wine glass, and a smaller glass for baijiu. Occasionally a small shallow dish is left for each diner, to hold a small amount of a condiment or sauce.

At homes and low-end restaurants, napkins are often paper tissues. High end restaurants usually provide cloth napkins.

Unlike some Western restaurants, salt, pepper, or sugar are not usually on the table, but soy sauce, vinegar, and hot sauce are. Black vinegar is popular in northern China as a dipping sauce, particularly for dumplings.

Dinner Menus

Ship: *Queen Mary 2*
Britannia Club

CANYON RANCH / SPA SELECTION
Appetizer – Rocket salad with roasted tomatoes
Chicken with a sausage meat stuffing served with carrots, steamed bok choy
Buttered rice and fig demi-glace
Dessert – Linzer cake with raspberry coulis

APPETIZERS AND SOUP
Baby prawn and 'grapefruit salad with Marie Rose sauce
Chicken liver parfait with red onion compote and toasted brioche
Thai vegetable spring rolls with rice noodle salad and tangy cashew sauce
Pumpkin soup with roasted seeds
Minestrone Genovese
Chilled apple and yoghurt soup

SALAD
Baby spinach, grapefruit, orange, pecan nuts and red onion
French vinaigrette or Marie Rose dressing

Entrees

Fettuccine with whisky and orange cured salmon, green peppercorns and chopped dill

Fillet of cod with snow peas and tomato, boiled potatoes, asparagus, cauliflower and a warm tomato and chervil vinaigrette

Roast leg of lamb with creamed savoy cabbage, roast pumpkin, lyonnaise potato and rosemary sauce

Seared sirloin steak with western fries, corn on the cob, green beans and bourbon barbecue sauce

Portobello mushroom with Provençal vegetables, cherry tomato sauce and mozzarella cheese

Twice-baked potato with refried beans, guacamole and salsa

Desserts

Chocolate marquise with bitter orange coulis

Bacardi lemon crème brûlée

Warm apple strudel with brandy sauce

Low sugar cranberry and pecan pie with vanilla sauce

Honey and ginger, coconut ice creams with champagne sorbet and mango sauce

A selection of British and international cheeses with bread, biscuits, chutney, dried fruit and nuts

RMS *Titanic*
First class dinner menu (April 14, 1912)

First course – Hors D'Oeuvres and Oysters

Second course – Consommé Olga Cream of Barley

Third course – Poached salmon with mousseline sauce, cucumbers

Fourth course – Filet mignon or sauté of Chicken, lyonnaise or Vegetable marrow farci

Fifth course – Lamb with mint sauce or Sirloin of beef with chateau potatoes, green peas, creamed carrots, boiled rice or Parmentier and boiled new potatoes

Sixth course – Punch romaine

Seventh course – Roast squab and cress

Eighth course – Cold asparagus vinaigrette

Ninth course – Pate de foie gras and celery

Tenth course – Waldorf Pudding or peaches in chartreuse jelly or chocolate and vanilla eclairs with French Ice cream

Highly Opinionated

Train: *Orient Express*
4 courses

Pan fried turbot steak with thinly sliced potato scales and truffle carpaccio Champagne sauce.

Roast fillet of lamb, coated with argan oil and sweet garlic, with an oriental spices' jus.

Zucchini, eggplants, sweet peppers and tomatoes flavored with lemon thyme

Tabbouleh and peppermint fresh leaves

Selection of fine cheeses

Mont-Blanc cake with candied chestnuts

Federal Bureau of Prisons
5 week rotating weekly menu
Week 5, Monday

Pepper steak or tofu stir fry
Steamed rice
Steamed broccoli
Whole wheat bread
Beverage

Roman dinner, AD 200

Meat, fish, broccoli, cereals, porridge of breadcrumbs and onions fried in oil and seasoned with vinegar and chickpeas.

Airline: Air France La Premiere

Beginning: Langoustines, Oscietra caviar, tangy citrus fruit and gentian drops and cream of chestnut and celeriac soup.

Starters: choice of duck foie gras and a mango and pineapple compote or scallop terrine with herb jelly, whipped cream with mascarpone.

Main options: Blanquette-style veal shank with carrots, confit farmhouse poultry salmis with mushrooms, juniper flavored jus, lobster fricassee with seasonal vegetables or risotto-style root vegetables, button mushrooms, porcini mushrooms and Beaufort cheese.

Salad: can create salad to accompany meal and then have a choice of cheeses and a dessert of Lenôtre Paris (dried fruit, nut and candied orange tartlet, almond and hazelnut cake).

Team Meal Before the Rose Bowl
Lawry's The Prime Rib, Beverly Hills, traditionally treats the two college football teams in what Lawry's calls the Beef Bowl

Salad
Prime rib of beef
Mashed potatoes and creamed corn
Apple pie a la mode

Onboard British Navy Ship in Napoleonic Era (circa 1803)

Stew was a typical dinnertime dish, consisting of boiled salted meat, onions and pepper mixed with ship's biscuit and stewed together. Supper at 4pm was usually a half pint of wine or a pint of grog with biscuit and cheese or butter.

The First Theme Restaurants

Café du Bagne (Café of the Penitentiary), Paris, France. Opened by Maxime Lisbonne in 1885 who had actually been in prison. Servers dressed as convicts with faux balls and chains on their legs.

Baron Long's Ship Café (Also known as Cabrillo's), 1905 – 1946. Venice Beach, California. "The Ship Café" was a replica of the Spanish galleon 'Cabrillo'. The Ship was built the same year as the Venice Pier. Both were destroyed by fire in 1920 and both rebuilt.

The Pirate's Cave, Greenwich Village, New York. 1916. A tearoom with a pirate theme.

Zulu Hut, Studio City, Los Angeles, California 1924–1931. Started by actor Raymond McKee. Its menu included cornpone, squab and fried chicken. There were no knives and no forks, customers had to eat with their hands.

The Jail Café, Los Angeles, California 1925. Resembled a stone jail complete with watchtower. Customers gathered around a large fireplace or could be served at a table in private cells by servers dressed as convicts. There were no knives and no forks, customers had to eat with their hands.

The Pirate's Den, Hollywood, California. Opened in 1940 and owned by Bob Hope, Bing Crosby, Rudy Vallee, Fred MacMurray, Errol Flynn, and Johnny Weissmuller. Servers dressed as, wait for it… Pirates! Naturally, the manager carried a bullwhip in case staff is not moving fast enough.

Countries With No McDonald's
Still locations available to grab a franchise!

Afghanistan	Albania	Algeria
Angola	Armenia	Bangladesh
Barbados	Belize	Benin
Bermuda	Bhutan	Bolivia
Botswana	Burkina Faso	Burundi
Cambodia	Cameroon	Cape Verde
Central African Republic	Chad	Comoros
Cook Islands	Congo	Democratic Republic of Congo
Djibouti	Dominica	East Timor
Equatorial Guinea		
Eritrea	Ethiopia	Gabon
Gambia	Ghana	Grenada
Guinea	Guinea-Bissau	Haiti
Iceland	Iran	Iraq
Ivory Coast	Jamaica	Kenya

The Restaurant Compendium for the Curious

Kiribati	Kyrgyzstan	Laos
Macedonia	Madagascar	Malawi
Maldives	Mali	Marshall Islands
Mauritius	Micronesia	Mongolia
Montenegro	Mozambique	Myanmar
Namibia	Nauru	Nepal
Niger	Nigeria	North Korea
Palau	Papua New Guinea	Rwanda
Saint Kitts and Nevis	Saint Lucia	Sao Tome and Principe
Senegal	Seychelles	Sierra Leone
Solomon Islands	Somalia	South Sudan
Sudan	Swaziland	Syria
Tajikistan	Togo	Tonga
Turkmenistan	Tuvalu	Uganda
Uzbekistan	Vanuatu	Vatican City
Yemen	Zimbabwe	

COUNTRIES WHERE FAST FOOD IS FORBIDDEN

Bermuda, Iran, Macedonia, North Korea, Yemen, and Zimbabwe

Highly Opinionated

Question:
How many restaurants have won the Malcolm Baldrige National Quality Award?

Answer:
Not many. Two to be exact.

What is it?
First of all, it's a big deal. Presented by the President of the United States, The Baldrige Program oversees the nation's only Presidential award for performance excellence. It includes categories of customer satisfaction and engagement, product and service outcomes and process, efficiency, workforce satisfaction and engagement, revenue and market share, and social responsibility

In hospitality, only two restaurants and one hotel have won
- Pal's Sudden Service (2001) Tennessee. Only makes one mistake every 3,000 orders.
- K & N Management (2010) Texas. Rudy's Country Store & Bar-B-Q and Mighty Fine Burgers, Fries and Shakes
- Ritz Carlton Hotels (1992 and 1999)

Oldest Restaurants in the World Still Operating

803 **St. Peter Stifts Kulinarium,** Salzburg, Austria. Columbus, Faust, and Mozart are believed to have dined here.

1146 **Wurstkuchl**, Regensburg, Germany.

1147 **The Old House**, Llangynwyd, Wales.

1153 **Ma Yu Ching's Bucket Chicken House,** Kaifeng, Henan, China. In 2007, Ma Yu Ching's bucket chicken was named "an intangible cultural heritage" of Henan Province.

1198 Ireland **The Brazen Head,** Usher's Quay, Dublin, Ireland.

1273 **Piwnica Swidnicka** (Świdnica Cellar in English), Wroclaw, Poland.

The Restaurant Compendium for the Curious

1345 La Couronne, Rouen, France. In 1948, the restaurant served chef and author Julia Child her first French meal.

1360 The Sheep Heid Inn, Edinburgh, Scotland. The Inn includes an old fashioned bowling alley, built around 1880.

1380 Hotel Gasthof Lowen, Liechtenstein.

1465 Honke Owariya, Kyoto, Japan.

1630 El M'Rabet, Tunisia.

1673 The White Horse Tavern, Newport, Rhode Island, USA.

1725 Sobrino de Botin. Madrid, Spain. It is said that a young Goya was employed as a dishwasher or maybe a waiter. Originally called Casa Botin, after the owner, Jean Botin, but after his death, a nephew renamed it to Sobrino de Botin. Sobrino is Spanish for nephew.

1801 Komagata Dozeu, Tokyo, Japan.

1816 La Puerta Falsa (The False Door), Bogota, Columbia. Best known for its ajiaco soup and its tamales.

1840 Asci Bacaksiz, Afyonkarahisar, Turkey.

1860 El Imparcia, Buenos Aires, Argentina.

Oldest Restaurants Still Operating In the US

1673 The White Horse Tavern, Newport, Rhode Island. Oldest operating tavern in the US and 10th oldest in the world. It is recognized as a National Historic Landmark. It has had only 9 owners in its 350-year history.

1728 Red Fox Inn, Middleburg, Virginia (originally Chinn's Ordinary). Oldest restaurant still operating in US. Listed on National Register of Historic Places.

1756 The Old '76 House, Tappan, New York.

Built in 1668, The '76 House is the oldest tavern in the US and oldest restaurant in New York.

1776 **The Griswold Inn**, Essex, Connecticut. One of oldest continuously run taverns in the US

1795 **Bell in Hand Tavern**, Boston, Massachusetts. One of the oldest continuously operated taverns in the US

1826 **Union Oyster House**, Boston, Massachusetts —Oldest continuously operated restaurant in Boston and among the oldest in the US

1837 **Delmonico's**, NYC, New York. America's first fine dining restaurant.

Oldest Restaurants in Each State

Alabama: The Bright Star, Bessemer, opened in 1907. Bon Appétit called it "one of America's best neighborhood restaurants." In 2010, the restaurant was awarded the James Beard American Classic Award.

Alaska: Peggy's, Anchorage. 1944.

Arizona: The Palace Restaurant and Saloon, Prescott. 1877

Arkansas: White House Café, Camden. 1907

Oark General Store, Oark. 1890

California: Tadich Grill, San Francisco. 1849

Colorado: The Buckhorn Exchange, Denver. 1893

Connecticut: The Griswold Inn, Essex. 1776

Delaware: Kelly's Logan House, Wilmington. 1864. Also, it is the oldest continuously run bar owned by the same family in the US

Florida: Columbia Restaurant, Tampa. 1905

Georgia: The Plaza Restaurant & Bar, Thomasville. 1916

Hawaii: Manago Hotel Restaurant, Captain Cook. 1917

Idaho: The Snake Pit, Kingston. 1879. It got its name from the water snakes that used to be in the swampy area around the outhouses

Illinois: The Village Tavern, Long Grove. 1847

Indiana: The Log Inn, Haubstadt. 1844

Iowa: Breitbach's Country Dining, Sherrill. 1852

Kansas: Hays House, Council Grove. 1857

Kentucky: Talbott Tavern, Bardstown. 1779

Louisiana, Antoine's Restaurant, New Orleans. 1840

Maine: The Palace Diner, Biddeford. 1927

Maryland: The Old South Mountain Inn, Boonsboro. 1732

Massachusetts: Union Oyster House, Boston. 1826

Warren Tavern, Charlestown, 1780

Michigan: The White Horse Inn, Metamora. 1850

Minnesota: Hubbel House, Mantorville 1854

Mississippi: Weidmann's Restaurant, Meridian. 1870. Each table is set with a handmade peanut butter crock and an assortment of crackers.

Missouri: J. Huston Tavern, Arrow Rock. 1834 Originally provided food and lodging for travelers along the Santa Fe Trail. The restaurant is run with a partnership with the Missouri State Parks and Friends of Arrow Rock.

Montana: Pekin Noodle Parlor, Butte. 1880, 1909, or 1916. Butte native Evel Knievel was a regular.

Nebraska: Glur's Tavern, Columbus. 1876. Buffalo Bill ate here in 1883. The building is listed on the National Register of Historic Places.

Nevada: The Martin Hotel, Winnemucca. 1898 (but, maybe between

1898 and 1908).

New Hampshire: The Fox Tavern at the Hancock Inn, Hancock. 1789

New Jersey: The Cranbury Inn, Cranbury. 1750

The Black Horse Tavern and Pub, Mendham 1742

New Mexico: El Farol, Santa Fe. In 1835, opened as La Cantina del Canon on Canyon Road. Changed name to El Farol in 1963.

New York: The '76 House, Tappan. 1668

North Carolina: Carolina Coffee Shop, Chapel Hill, next to the UNC campus. 1922

North Dakota: Peacock Alley American Grill and Bar, Bismarck. 1933 right after prohibition.

Ohio: The Golden Lamb, Lebanon. 1803.

Oklahoma: Cattlemen's Steakhouse, Oklahoma City. 1910. Owner Hank Frey put up Cattlemen's in a bet with Gene Wade that he could not roll a 'hard six,' (two 3s). Wade put up his life savings and with one roll of the dice, Gene Wade owned the restaurant. The '33' brand on the wall became a well-known symbol of Wade's good luck.

Oregon: Huber's Café, Portland. 1879. Started as the Bureau Saloon

Pennsylvania: McGillin's Olde Ale House, Philadelphia. 1860. Originally called the Bell in Hand Tavern. In 2013, *Gourmet* magazine called McGillin's one of the 3 coolest bars in the United States

Rhode Island: White Horse Tavern, Newport. 1673. Also oldest bar and restaurant in US.

South Carolina: Henry's House, Charleston. 1932

South Dakota: Legends Steakhouse in the Silverado Franklin Hotel, Deadwood. Opened in 1903.

Tennessee: Varallo's Chili Parlor and Restaurant, Nashville. 1907

Texas: Scholz Garten, Austin. 1866 founded by a German immigrant/Civil War veteran who wanted a place for the German community of Austin to gather and enjoy traditional food and beer.

Utah: Idle Isle Café, Brigham City, 1921

Vermont: Ye Olde Tavern, Manchester. 1790

Virginia: The Red Fox Inn & Tavern, Middleburg. 1728

Washington: Horseshoe Café, Bellingham. Opened in 1886 where people came for jobs in logging, coal mining, and fishing.

Washington DC: Old Ebbitt Grill, 1856. It became Washington's first known saloon. Presidents William McKinley, Ulysses S. Grant, Andrew Johnson, Grover Cleveland, and Theodore Roosevelt have all dined here.

West Virginia: North End Tavern & Brewery, Parkersburg. 1899

Wisconsin: Red Circle Inn & Bistro, Nashotah. 1847

Wyoming: Miners & Stockmen's Steakhouse & Spirits, Hartville. 1862

Restaurants on the US National Register of Historic Places

Authorized by the National Historic Preservation Act of 1966, the National Park Service's National Register of Historic Places identifies, evaluates, and protects America's historic and archeological resources. There are more than 96,000 total properties listed in the National Register.

*Open

ALASKA

Black Rapids Roadhouse, Delta Junction, Alaska. 1902 – 1993. One of last remaining roadhouses on the Valdez to Fairbanks Trail. Currently being restored by nearby Lodge at Black Rapids

*Ricka's Landing Roadhouse, Big Delta, Alaska,1898. Now operated as a museum.

Spring Creek Lodge, Anchorage, Alaska, 1849-1974. Placed in Register in recognition of its contributions to the cultural heritage of Alaska

ARKANSAS
*Butchie's Drive-in (Bailey's Dairy Treat now), Hot Springs, Arkansas 1952. Currently operating as Bailey's Dairy Treat.

Opal's Steakhouse, Hot Springs, Arkansas, 1948. Art Moderne style. In 1952, changed name to the Golden Drumstick Restaurant, then changed to clothing store, furniture store, and laundromat.

CALIFORNIA
*The French Laundry, Yountville, California.

*Roy's Motel and Café, Amboy, California, 1938. On Route 66, example of roadside Mid-Century Modern Googie architecture.

COLORADO
Buckhorn Exchange, Denver, Colorado 1893

The Fort, Morrison, Colorado

The Red Onion, Aspen, Colorado 1892

FLORIDA
Driftwood Inn and Restaurant, Vero Beach, Florida 1937

S & S Sandwich Shop, Miami, Florida, 1938

HAWAII
*Salvation Army Wai'oli Tea Room, Honolulu, Hawaii, 1922-2014, reopened in 2018 as the Wai'oli Kitchen and Bake Shop.

ILLINOIS
Ariston Café, Litchfield, Illinois. 1935

Belvidere Café, Motel, and gas station, Litchfield, Illinois 1929

Milk Pail Restaurant, Dundee Township, Illinois. 1926

INDIANA
Indianapolis White Castle, Indianapolis, Indiana, 1927

Slippery Noodle Inn, Indianapolis, Indiana, 1850

KANSAS
Rosberg-Holmgren-Clareen Block, Lindsborg, Kansas, 1909

KENTUCKY
*Harland Sanders Café and Museum, Corbin, Kentucky. Colonel Sanders operated it from 1940-1956.

MARYLAND
*Brooklandville House (Valley Inn), Brooklandville, Maryland 1832

MASSACHUSETTS
Locke-Ober, Boston, Massachusetts, 1875. This was in the movie Good Will Hunting.

MINNESOTA
*Naniboujou Club Lodge, Cook County, Minnesota 1929. Named for a Cree spirit of legend and the lodge has a Cree theme to its décor.

While Castle Building No. 8, Minneapolis, Minnesota, 1936. This is an example of the manufactured, movable, prefab structures assembled on site that White Castle used for years.

MISSISSIPPI
*Weidmann's Restaurant, Meridian, Mississippi, 1870

Oldest restaurant in Mississippi.

MISSOURI
*Savoy Hotel and Grill, Kansas City, Missouri, 1903. It is the oldest continuously operated restaurant in Kansas City. Booth No. 4 is known as the presidents' booth with Warren Harding, Harry S. Truman, Gerald Ford, and Ronald Reagan all having eaten here.

MONTANA
*Lake McDonald Lodge Coffee Shop, Glacier National Park, Montana, 1965. In 2018, renamed Jammer Joe's, after a Red Bus driver who gave tours in the park.

Matt's Place Drive-in, Butte, Montana 1930

NEVADA
The Green Shack, Las Vegas, Nevada, 1929 – 1999. Originally named the Colorado, then the Swanky Club.

NEW JERSEY
*Peacock Inn, Princeton, New Jersey, 1911

NEW YORK
*Gage and Tollner, Brooklyn, New York, 1879. The NYC Landmarks Preservation Commission granted Gage & Tollner both individual and interior landmark status; it is only the third space to be designated as an interior landmark (the other two are the NY Public Library and Grant's Tomb) and the only standalone restaurant in NYC history to hold both designations.

*Walter's Hot Dog Stand, Mamaroneck, New York, 1919

NORTH CAROLINA
S&W Cafeteria, Charlotte, North Carolina, 1920

NORTH DAKOTA
*The Kegs, Grand Forks, North Dakota, 1935

OHIO
Pal*Bender's Tavern, Canton, Ohio 1899

*Mecklenburg's Garden, Cincinnati, Ohio. 1865. Originally, the Mount Auburn Gardens & Billiards Saloon, now a German restaurant and biergarten.

OKLAHOMA
Elks Victory Lodge and Ruby's Grill, Oklahoma City, Oklahoma, 1929

OREGON
*Huber's, Portland, Oregon 1879. Originally, the Bureau Saloon.

*Jake's Famous Crawfish, Portland, Oregon 1892

PENNSYLVANIA
Lynn Hall, Port Allegany, Pennsylvania. In operation from from 1935-1950's

TEXAS
*Fossati's Deli – Victoria, Texas. 1882. Oldest deli in Texas. Still owned and operated by the same family.

*U-Drop Inn, Shamrock, Texas, 1936. Also, a Texas Historic Landmark. An example of Art Deco.

UTAH
*Kanab Lodge, Kanab, Utah, 1885. Now called Jake's Chaparral.

VERMONT
Dog Team Tavern, Middlebury, Vermont. 1936

VIRGINIA
***Carl's Ice Cream**, Fredericksburg, Virginia. An example of Art Moderne

***Red Fox Inn**, Middleburg

WASHINGTON DC 1923
1923 *Billy Simpson's House of Seafood and Steaks. Now called "the French Bistro Chez Billy

Highly Opinionated Restaurants That You Need to Try

ALABAMA
The Bright Star, Bessemer

Big Bob Gibson, Decatur

Archibald's BBQ, Northport

Chris' Hotdogs, Montgomery

Highlands Bar and Grill, Birmingham

ALASKA
Homestead Restaurant, Homer

Talkeetna Roadhouse, Talkeetna

ARIZONA
Palace Restaurant and Saloon, Prescott

Sugar Bowl, Scottsdale,

CALIFORNIA
Alice's Restaurant, Berkeley

The French Laundry, Yountville

In-N-Out Burger, many locations

Polo Lounge, Los Angeles

Spago, Beverly Hills

Swan Oyster Depot, San Francisco

Tadich Grill, San Francisco

COLORADO
Buckhorn Exchange, Denver

CONNECTICUT
Louis Lunch, New Haven

Mystic Pizza, Mystic

DELAWARE
Jessop's Tavern, New Castle

FLORIDA
Berne's Steakhouse, Tampa

Joe's Stone Crab, Miami Beach

Columbia Restaurant, Tampa

GEORGIA
Atkins Park, Atlanta

The Colonade, Atlanta

The Varsity, Atlanta

Mrs. Wilke's Dining Room, Savannah

HAWAII
Mama's Fish House, Maui

IDAHO
Beverly's, Coeur d'Alene

ILLINOIS
Alinea, Chicago

Lou Malnati's, Chicago

Portillo's, Chicago

INDIANA
St. Elmo Steak House, Indianapolis

IOWA
Canteen Lunch in the Alley, Ottumwa

KANSAS
The Cozy Inn, Salina

KENTUCKY
The Brown Hotel, Louisville

LOUISIANA
Antoine's, New Orleans

Arnaud's, New Orleans

Café Du Monde, New Orleans

Commander's Palace, New Orleans

MAINE
Five Islands, Lobster Co., Georgetown

MARYLAND
Faidley Seafood, Baltimore

MASSACHUSETTS
Union Oyster House, Boston

MICHIGAN
Golden Harvest Restaurant, Lansing

Sleder's, Traverse City

Weber's Restaurant, Ann Arbor

MINNESOTA
Matt's Bar and Grill, Minneapolis

MISSISSIPPI
Ajax Diner, Oxford

MISSOURI
Arthur Bryant's, Kansas City

MONTANA
Polebridge Mercantile, Polebridge

NEBRASKA
The Drover, Omaha

NEVADA
The Golden Steer, Las Vegas

NEW HAMPSHIRE
Pickity Place, Mason

NEW JERSEY
Tops Diner, East Newark

HIGHLY OPINIONATED

NEW MEXICO
    Café Pasqual's, Santa Fe

    Downtown Subscription, Santa Fe

    Geronimo, Santa Fe

    Pie-O-Neer Pies, Pie Town

    Rancho de Chimayo, Chimayo

    Campo at Los Poblanos, Albuquerque

NEW YORK
    Delmonico's, NYC

    Fraunces Tavern, NYC

    Jean Georges, NYC

    Katz's Deli, NYC

    Keens Steakhouse, NYC

    Peter Luger Steakhouse, Brooklyn

    Prince Street Pizza, Manhattan

    Sylvia's, Brooklyn

NORTH CAROLINA
    The Angus Barn, Raleigh

NORTH DAKOTA
    Wurst Bier Hall, Fargo

OHIO
    Camp Washington Chili, Cincinnati

    Schmidt's Sausage Haus

OKLAHOMA
Cattlemen's Steakhouse, Oklahoma City

OREGON
Huber's Café, Portland

Jake's Famous Crawfish, Portland

Voodoo Doughnut, Portland

PENNSYLVANIA
City Tavern, Philadelphia

Geno's Steaks, Philadelphia

McGillan's Olde Alehouse, Philadelphia

Pat's King of Steaks, Philadelphia

Ralph's Italian Restaurant, Philadelphia

Primanti Bros., Pittsburgh

RHODE ISLAND
Matunuck Oyster Bar, South Kingston

White Horse Tavern, Newport

SOUTH CAROLINA
Husk, Charleston

SOUTH DAKOTA
Alpine Inn, Hill City

TENNESSEE
Bluebird Café, Nashville

Gus's World-Famous Fried Chicken, Memphis

TEXAS
Salt Lick BBQ, Driftwood

Snow's BBQ, Lexington

UTAH
Red Iguana, Salt Lake City

VERMONT
Hen of the Wood, Waterbury

VIRGINIA
The Inn at Little Washington, Washington

Red Fox Inn and Tavern, Middleburg

WASHINGTON
Maneki, Seattle

WASHINGTON DC
Old Ebbitt Grill

Ben's Chili Bowl

WEST VIRGINIA
Hillbilly Hot Dogs, Lesage

WISCONSIN
L' Etoile, Madison

Frank's Diner, Kenosha

WYOMING
The Irma, Cody

What Do All Those Letters Mean on the Chef's Coat?

Chef Certifications

ACF (American Culinary Federation)
CFC – Certified Fundamentals Cook
CC - Certified Culinarian
CSC - Certified Sous Chef
CCC – Certified Chef de Cuisine
CEC – Certified Executive Chef
CMC – Certified Master Chef
PCC – Personal Certified Chef
PCEC – Personal Certified Executive Chef
CCA – Certified Culinary Administrator
CCE – Certified Culinary Educator

International Food Service Executives Association
CFM – Certified Food Manager
MCFE – Master Certified Food Executive
CFE – Certified Food Executive
CFA – Certified Food Associate (high school students)

National Registry of Food Safety Professionals
FSMC - Food Safety Manager Certification
FHC - Food Handler Certificate

American Hotel & Lodging Educational Institute (AHLAEI)
CHE – Certified Hospitality Educator
CHI – Certified Hospitality Instructor
CHPM – Certified Hospitality Purchasing Manager
CHDT – Certified Hospitality Department Trainer
CHS – Certified Hospitality Supervisor
CME – Certified Maintenance Employee
CRDE – Certified Rooms Division Executive
CLSD – Certified Lodging Security Director
CLSS – Certified Lodging Security Supervisor

CHT – Certified Hospitality Trainer
CHA – Certified Hotel Administrator
CFBE – Certified Food and Beverage Executive
CGSP – Certified Guest Service Professional
CHFE – Certified Hospitality Facilities Executive
CHHE – Certified Hospitality Housekeeping Executive
CHRM – Certified Hospitality Revenue Manager
CHS – Certified Hospitality Supervisor
CHSP – Certified Hospitality Sales Professional
CHDT – Certified Hospitality Department Trainer
CMM – Certified Meeting Management
CBA – Certified Breakfast Attendant
CFDR – Certified Front Desk Representative
CGA – Certified Guestroom Attendant
CKC – Certified Kitchen Cook
CME – Certified Maintenance Employee
CRS – Certified Restaurant Server
CHIA – Certification in Hotel Industry Analytics

SIZE MATTERS
World's Largest Full-Service Restaurants

Bawabet Dimashq Restaurant (Damascus Gate Restaurant), Damascus, Syria has 6,014 seats, and 580,000 square foot dining area

The Royal Dragon Restaurant, Bangkok, Thailand. Covers 8.35 acres, the open-air restaurant can seat 5,000 diners and offers more than 1,000 dishes.

West Lake Restaurant, Changsha, China has more than 5,000 seats. Employs 300 chefs and 1,000 employees.

Zehnder's Restaurant, Frakenmuth, Michigan can seat 1,500. Built in 1856.

La Felicita, Paris, France. 48,500 square feet, 8 kitchens, 9 chefs, and

3 bars. Seats 1,000.

Columbia Restaurant, Tampa, Florida. Started in 1905. 52,000 square feet, seats up to 1,700 customers in 15 dining rooms and takes up one city block.

The Varsity, Atlanta, Georgia. This drive-in restaurant can accommodate 600 cars outside and 800 customers inside.

Deeper Dive
Food Truck

The first food truck was probably the chuck wagon, invented by cattleman Colonel Charles Goodnight (1836-1929). Cattle drives could be as long as a thousand miles and take 4 or 5 months without any towns along the way. Goodnight wanted the best cowboys and to get the best cowboys, he had to feed them well, so he rebuilt an Army surplus wagon and equipped it with cabinets, shelves, and drawers to hold food, utensils, added a hinged worktop for prep, with a large water barrel on the side. Others began making and selling chuck wagons, including Studebaker. The chuck wagon was used as late as the 1930s and now its back. Today's food truck still has 4 wheels, but a different motor.

Goodnight's wagon came to be known as the Chuck wagon probably because of Charles being shortened to Chuck or because cowboys used to call their meals "chuck."

HIGHLY OPINIONATED

I'll Drink to That!

CHEERS!

Traditional toasts around the world

Australia: Cheers, big ears...Same goes, big nose (Cheers!)
Belgium: Sante! (To you!)
Canada: Cheers! (Cheers!)
China: Gān Bēi! (Empty the cup!)   Kai pay! (Drain your glass!)
England: Cheers! (Cheers!)
Finland: Kippis! (Cheers!)
France: Sante! (To your health) or Tchin Tchin (Cheers!)
Germany: Prost! (Good health!) or Zum Wohl! (Good health!)
Greece: Ya Mas! (To our health!) or Stinygiasou! (To your health!)
Guatemala: Salud! (To your health!)
Hungary: Egészségére! (For our health!)
Iceland: Skál! (Bowl!)
Ireland: Sláinte (Cheers!)
Israel: L'chaim! (To life!)
Italy: Cincin! Or Salute! (To your health!)
Japan: Kanpai! (Empty the glass!)
Mexico: Salud! (Health)
Netherlands: Proost! (Cheers!)
Panama: Salud! (Health!)
Philippines: Mabuhay! (Long life!)
Poland: Na zdrowia! (To your health!)
Portugal: Saude! (To your health!)

Russia: Za zdoróvie! (To your health!)
South Korea: Gun Bae! (Empty the glass!)
Spain: Salud! (Good health!)
Sweden: Skål! (Cheers!)
Thailand: Chone Gaow! (Cheers!) or Chai yo! (Good luck!)
Turkey: Serefe! (Cheers!)
Ukraine: Bud-mo! (To your health!) Za Vas! (here's to you!)
United States: Cheers! (Cheers!)
Vietnam: Môt Hai Ba, Yo! (One, two, three, cheers!)

Toasts

Here's to staying positive and testing negative

May we be who our dogs think we are

May you live as long as you like,
    And have all you like as long as you live

I would rather be with the people in this room than with the finest
    people I know

Here's to those who wish us well, all the rest can go to hell

Here's to doing and drinking, not sitting and thinking

May we all have the chance to prove that money can't make us happy

Here's to all the days that end in "y"

Here's to the nights we'll never remember
    With our friends, we'll never forget

May we get what we want, but never what we deserve

Here's to the man who is wisest and best
    Here's to the man who with judgment is blest,

> Here's to the man who's as smart as can be
> I drink to the man who agrees with me!

Eat, drink and be merry, for tomorrow we diet

You're born in pain, you live in fear, you die alone, Merry Christmas

May you never forget what is worth remembering or remember what is best forgotten

To clean glasses and old corks

May you live for as long as you want, and never want for as long as you live!

To your very good health. May you live to be as old as your jokes

May your home always be too small to hold all your friends

May the winds of fortune sail you;

may you sail a gentle sea,

may it always be the other guy who says: "This drink's on me."

May we live to learn well
    And learn to live well.

Here's to friends and family who know us well, but love us just the same

May the roof above us never fall in,
    And may we friends gathered below
    Never fall out

Here's to bread, for without bread, there'd be no toast

Some ships are wooden ships, but those ships may sink.
    The best ships are friendships, and to those ships, we drink

Wise, kind, gentle, generous, sexy. But enough about me, here's to you

To us: for this is the youngest we'll ever be and the oldest we've been

To the fall of the Roman Empire, may ours be just as memorable

May the best of your past be the worse of your future

May misfortune follow you the rest of your life,
    And never catch up

Oldies but goodies:

Down the hatch

Bottoms up

One for the road

Raise a glass!

Wine Bottle Sizes

Split (piccolo) ¼ standard bottle or 1 5-ounce glass
Half (demi) ½ standard bottle or 2.5 glasses
Half-liter (jennie) ⅔ of standard bottle or 3 glasses
Standard 1 standard bottle or 5 glasses
Liter 1 ⅓ standard bottle or 7 glasses
Magnum 2 standard bottles or 10 glasses
Jeroboam (double magnum) 4 standard bottles or 20 glasses
Rehoboam 6 standard bottles or 30 glasses
Methuselah (Imperial) 8 standard bottles or 40 glasses
Salmanazar A full case of 12 standard bottles or 60 glasses
Balthazar 16 standard bottles or 80 glasses
Nebuchadnezzar 20 standard bottles or 100 glasses
Melchior 2 full cases of 24 standard bottles or 120 glasses
Solomon 26 standard bottles or 130 glasses
Sovereign 35 standard bottles or 175 glasses

Primat (Goliath) 36 standard bottles or 180 glasses

Melchizedek (Midas) The largest bottle in the world, 40 standard bottles or 200 glasses

States Where a Minor Can Legally Drink in a Restaurant if Served by Parent or Guardian

Texas - if drinks are in the visible presence of the minor's adult parent, guardian, or spouse.

Louisiana - if the underage person is accompanied by a parent or guardian who is at least 21 years old.

Mississippi - underage people who are at least 18 years old are allowed to consume light wine or beer with the consent and presence of their parent or legal guardian. Underage people who are at least 18 and serving in the US armed services "may lawfully possess and consume light wine or beer on military property where the consumption of light wine or beer is allowed.

Nevada - if the underage person is accompanied by a parent or guardian who is at least 21 years old.

Ohio - if it is in the visible presence of the minor's adult parent, guardian, or spouse.

Wisconsin - if accompanied by parent or legal guardian.

Wyoming - if it is done in the physical presence of a parent or legal guardian.

Countries With No Minimum Legal Drinking Age
(8 countries)
Burkina Faso, Cameroon, Guinea-Bissau, Kosovo, Mali, Sao Tome and Principe, Timor-Leste, Togo

Countries Where Minimum Legal Drinking Age is Between 10 and 15 Years Old
(2 countries)
Antigua and Barbuda, Central African Republic

Countries Where Minimum Legal Drinking Age is Between 16 and 17 Years Old
(21 countries)
Austria, Belgium, Burundi, Congo, Cyprus, Denmark, Dominica, Germany, Grenada, Guyana, Haiti, Liechtenstein, Luxembourg, Malta, Morocco, Portugal, Saint Lucia, Saint Vincent and the Grenadines, San Marino, Spain, Switzerland

Countries Where Minimum Legal Drinking Age is Between 18 and 19 Years Old
(118 countries)
Albania, Algeria, Andorra, Angola, Argentina, Armenia, Australia, Azerbaijan, Bahamas, Barbados, Belarus, Belize, Bhutan, Bolivia, Bosnia and Herzegovina, Botswana, Brazil, Bulgaria, Canada, Cape Verde, Chad, Chile, *China, Colombia, Comoros, Costa Rica, Croatia, Cuba, Czech Republic, Democratic Republic of the Congo, Dominican Republic, Ecuador, Egypt, El Salvador, Eritrea, Estonia, Ethiopia, Fiji, Finland, France, Gambia, Gabon, Georgia, Ghana, Greece, Guatemala, Guinea, Honduras, Hungary, India, Ireland, Israel, Italy, Jamaica, Jordan, Kazakhstan, Kenya, Kyrgyzstan, Laos, Latvia, Lesotho, Liberia, Lithuania, Macao, Macedonia, Madagascar, Malawi, Malaysia, Mauritius, Mexico, Moldova, Monaco, Montenegro, Mozambique, Myanmar, Namibia, Nepal, Netherlands, New Zealand, Nicaragua, Niger, Nigeria, Norway, Panama, Papua New Guinea, Peru, Philippines, Poland, Romania, Russia, Rwanda, Saint Kitts and Nevis, Senegal, Serbia, Seychelles, Sierra Leone, Singapore, Slovakia, Slovenia, South Africa, South Korea, Suriname, Swaziland, Sweden, Syria, Tajikistan, Tanzania, Tonga, Trinidad and Tobago, Tunisia, Turkey, Turkmenistan, Tuvalu, Uganda, Ukraine, United Kingdom, Uruguay, Vanuatu, Vatican City, Venezuela, Vietnam, Zambia, Zimbabwe

Countries Where Minimum Legal Drinking Age is 20 Years Old
(6 countries)
Benin, Iceland, Japan, Paraguay, Thailand, Uzbekistan

Countries Where Minimum Legal Drinking Age is 21 Years Old
(15 countries)
Cambodia, Côte d'Ivoire, Equatorial Guinea, Indonesia, Iraq, Kiribati, Micronesia, Mongolia, Nauru, Oman, Palau, Solomon Islands, Samoa, Sri Lanka, United States

Countries Where it is Illegal to Drink at Any Age
(16 countries)
Afghanistan, Bahrain, Bangladesh, Brunei Darussalam, Iran, Kuwait, Libya, Maldives, Mauritania, Pakistan, Qatar, Saudi Arabia, Somalia, Sudan, United Arab Emirates, Yemen

Legal Drinking US Constitutional Amendments

18th amendment (January 16, 1919): Section 1: After one year from the ratification of this article the manufacture, sale, or transportation of intoxicating liquors within, the importation thereof into, or the exportation thereof from the United States and all territory subject to the jurisdiction thereof for beverage purposes is hereby prohibited.

21st amendment (Ratified December 5, 1933): Section 1 The eighteenth article of amendment to the Constitution of the United States is hereby repealed. This amendment ended national prohibition.

What the Heck is BAC?

It is a test for drunk driving. Blood Alcohol Concentration (BAC) limit is how much alcohol can be in the blood.

In the United States, the maximum is 0.08 for drivers over 21. A

BAC of 0.08 means there are eight units of alcohol for every 10,000 units of blood.

For comparison, most European countries have a BAC limit of 0.05. That's about one beer or one small glass of wine.

According to the Cleveland Clinic, Alcohol (ethyl alcohol or ethanol) is the intoxicating ingredient found in beer, wine and liquor. When you drink a beverage that contains alcohol, your stomach and small intestines rapidly absorb the alcohol and enters into your bloodstream. Alcohol is a toxin, so your liver metabolizes the alcohol to filter it out of your blood.

If you're drinking faster than your liver can process the alcohol, your BAC increases and you may feel intoxicated. In general, your liver can process about one alcoholic drink per hour. One alcoholic drink is typically defined as 12 ounces of beer, 5 ounces of wine or 1.5 ounces of liquor.

Dram Shop Liability (state law, not federal)

Dram shop liability is a big deal to restaurants and bars. If a customer buys a drink, leaves the bar/restaurant, and then gets into an accident, the owner of the place where the drink was served is legally responsible. All states have some form of dram shop laws.

There are two main types of dram shop cases, first party and third-party.

First-Party Dram Shop Cases

A "first party" dram shop case is when the injured party is the same person who got drunk. Some states do not allow first party dram shop cases because they think that people should be responsible for their own actions.

There is one major exception: If a minor child is served at an establishment, gets drunk, and gets injured, juries will often hold the establishment responsible.

Third-Party Dram Shop Cases

This happens when the injured person is someone *other* than the drunk person. The person hit by a drunk driver who got drunk at an establishment, might have a third-party dram shop case against the establishment.

Why is 'proof' *and* percentage of alcohol on bottles of distilled spirits?

In most of the world, alcohol content is measured by the percentage of alcohol in the liquid ('alcohol by volume' or ABV), even though proof is still found on labels.

In the US in 1848, the word proof was defined to mean twice the alcohol (ethanol) by volume (ABV). For example, a liquor with 50% alcohol is 100-proof and 80-proof would mean 40% of the liquid is alcohol.

Naturally, there are several stories that gave birth to the word proof.

One is that it came about in the 18th century when traders figured out the strength of the liquor by putting a match to a mix of liquor and gunpowder. If the mixture ignited, the traders had "proof" that at least half was alcohol.

The second story was that the king of England taxed high alcohol content higher than lower alcohol content, with the king getting more taxes if the mix of gunpowder and alcohol ignited.

Why Do Different Drinks Have Different Glasses?

Different glasses help the aroma and helps maintain the proper temperature so that the drink looks and tastes the best.

Red wine glasses have a larger bowl than white wine for easy swirling, to properly aerate, and to have the most aroma. They have long stems to hold so that the hand doesn't warm the drink.

White wine glasses are more slender than red wine glasses to help keep the temperature cool. It has a long stem to hold the drink keeping the hand away from the wine that would cause the temperature to warm up.

The Moscow Mule is traditionally served in a copper mug so that the mug stays really, really cold.

Martini glasses have large stems to help control the temperature of the drink since it never has ice in it. The wide opening provides a large surface area for aroma.

Rocks glass (old fashioned or lowball). The glass is perfect for ice cubes with plenty of room to stir. Usually for drinks that have more alcohol than mixer.

Champagne flute: Champagne is always served in a flute. Flutes are narrow to help preserve and display the bubbles. Since aroma is not as important as preserving bubbles, it has a smaller opening.

Highball glasses (Collins) are for tall cocktails that use ice cubes and contain more mixer than alcohol.

Snifter glasses, like brandy snifters, have large, round bottoms meant to be cradled in the hand so that the contents are gently warmed.

Hurricane glasses came about when Pat O'Brien put his signature drinks into hurricane lamp-shaped glasses.

Pilsner glasses are meant to show off the color of the beer.

Minimum Ages for Bartenders and Servers in Each State

Alabama Bartenders must be 21 to serve beer, wine, and spirits. Servers must be 19.

Alaska Bartenders and servers must be 21 to serve beer, wine, and spirits.

Arizona Servers and bartenders must be 19 to serve beer, wine, and spirits.

Arkansas Servers must be 19 and bartenders required to be 21 to serve beer, wine, and spirits.

California Bartenders must be 21 to serve beer, wine, and spirits.

Colorado Bartenders and servers must be 18 to serve beer, wine, and spirits.

Connecticut Bartenders and servers must be 18 to serve beer, wine, and spirits.

Delaware Servers must be 19 and bartenders need to be 21 to serve beer, wine, and spirits.

DC Bartenders must be 21 to serve beer, wine, and spirits. Servers must be 18.

Florida Bartenders and servers must be 18 to serve beer, wine, and spirits.

Highly Opinionated

Georgia Bartenders and servers must be 18 to serve beer, wine, and spirits.

Hawaii Bartenders and servers must be 18 to serve beer, wine, and spirits.

Idaho Bartenders and servers must be 19 to serve beer, wine, and spirits.

Illinois Bartenders and servers must be 18 to serve beer, wine, and spirits.

Indiana BAC limit 0.02 for drivers under age 21. Bartenders must be 21 to serve beer, wine, and spirits. Servers must be 19.

Iowa Bartenders and servers must be 18 to serve beer, wine, and spirits.

Kansas Bartenders and servers must be 18 to serve beer, wine, and spirits.

Kentucky Bartenders and servers must be 20 to serve beer, wine, and spirits.

Louisiana Bartenders and servers must be 18 to serve beer, wine, and spirits.

Maine Bartenders and servers must be 17 to serve beer, wine, and spirits.

Maryland Bartenders and servers must be 18 to serve beer and wine. Servers must be 18 to serve spirits and bartenders must be 21 to serve spirits.

Massachusetts Bartenders and servers must be 18 to serve beer, wine, and spirits.

Michigan Bartenders and servers must be 18 to serve beer, wine, and spirits.

Minnesota Bartenders and servers must be 18 to serve beer and wine. Servers must be 18 to serve Spirits and bartenders must be 21 to serve spirits.

Mississippi Bartenders must be 21 to serve beer, wine, and spirits. Servers must be 18.

Missouri Bartenders must be 21 to serve beer, wine, and spirits.

Montana Bartenders and servers must be 18 to serve beer, wine and

The Restaurant Compendium for the Curious

spirits.

Nebraska Bartenders and servers must be 19 to beer, wine, or spirits.

Nevada Servers and bartenders must be 21 to serve beer, wine, or spirits.

New Hampshire Servers and bartenders must be 18 to serve beer, wine, or spirits.

New Jersey Servers must be 19 to beer, wine, or spirits and bartenders must be 21.

New Mexico Servers must be 19 to beer, wine, or spirits and bartenders must be 21.

New York Servers must be 18 to serve beer, wine, or spirits and bartenders must be 21.

North Carolina Servers must be 18 to serve beer, wine, or spirits and bartenders must be 21. BAC limit 0.00 for drivers under age 21.

North Dakota Servers must be 18 to serve beer, wine, or spirits and bartenders must be 21.

Ohio Servers must be 19 and bartenders must be 21 to serve beer, wine, or spirits.

Oklahoma Servers must be 18 and bartenders must be 21 to serve beer, wine, or spirits.

Oregon Servers and bartenders must be 18 to serve beer, wine, or spirits.

Pennsylvania Servers and bartenders must be 18 to serve beer, wine, or spirits.

Rhode Island Servers and bartenders must be 18 to serve beer, wine, or spirits.

South Carolina. Servers must be 18 and bartenders must be 21 to serve beer, wine, or spirits.

South Dakota Servers and bartenders must be 18 to serve beer, wine, or spirits.

Tennessee Servers and bartenders must be 18 to serve beer, wine, or spirits.

Texas Servers and bartenders must be 21 to serve beer, wine, or spirits.

Utah Servers and bartenders must be 21 to serve beer, wine, or spirits.

Vermont Servers and bartenders must be 18 to serve beer, wine, or spirits.

Virginia Servers must be 18 and bartenders must be 21 to serve beer, wine, or spirits.

Washington Servers must be 18 and bartenders must be 21 to serve beer, wine, or spirits.

West Virginia Servers and bartenders must be 18 to serve beer, wine, or spirits.

Wisconsin Servers and bartenders must be 18 to serve beer, wine, or spirits.

Wyoming Servers must be 18 and bartenders must be 21 to serve beer, wine, or spirits.

50 Unusual Alcohol Laws in Each State
The Top 5
You can't make this up

#1 **Maine** – Cannot purchase alcoholic beverages until 9 o'clock on Sundays, *except* when St. Patrick's Day falls on a Sunday.

#2 **Missouri** - It's illegal to sit on the curb of any city street and drink beer from a bucket

#3 **Utah**- requires bars to have a sign that says, wait for it...'This is a Bar'.

#4 **Ohio** – No alcohol advertising can represent, portray, or make any reference to Santa Claus. They don't want children to associate drinking with Santa Claus. And start drinking. Really.

#5 **Texas** - In LeFors, Texas, it is illegal to take more than 3 drinks (sips or swallows) of a beer while standing up. My question: "Who is the designated counter?"

The Other 45

Alabama – Cannot advertise alcohol with neon signs

Colorado - A horse is considered a vehicle in the state meaning you can get a DUI if found 'driving' a horse drunk.

Delaware - Alcohol is not allowed to be served in clubs where there is also dancing.

Hawaii – If a minor gets a DWI, their parent or guardian will be the one required to go to an educational alcohol abuse class.

Iowa - Customers are allowed to start a tab at a bar, but bartenders must make sure tabs have been paid in full before customers leave.

Louisiana – Bars can be open 24/7 and it is legal to have drive-thru alcohol sales. Drinking in public is legal.

Massachusetts – No happy hour specials and no drinking games allowed

Nevada – It is not illegal to be publicly drunk. Bars can stay open 24 hours per day.

New Jersey – If you get a DUI, you are disqualified from receiving a personalized license plate

New Mexico - Public intoxication is not a crime in New Mexico. The state treats, instead of prosecutes those drunk in public. However, driving while intoxicated *is* a crime.

New York – Cannot serve alcoholic beverages until 10:00 o'clock Sundays.

Utah and Indiana – Restaurant customers can only buy drinks if they buy food.

Utah – Happy hour drink specials are illegal.

Utah – Until 2017, restaurants were required to have a 7-foot barrier around the bar to prevent children (gasp) from seeing the mixing and pouring of drinks.

Utah – May have the toughest drinking laws in the US. The BAC is 0.05, rather than the more common 0.08

Virginia – Cannot serve 2-for-1 drink specials

The ABCs of DWIs

- DWAI – means "driving while ability impaired" and in Colorado, if your BAC is .05 or more you will be arrested.
- OUI and OWI – "operating under the influence" and "operating while intoxicated."
- OMVI – (Operating Motor Vehicle Impaired). Ohio uses this term exclusively and has done away with the terms UI and DWI. Regardless of the term it means driving over the legal limit with alcohol or a controlled substance in your blood.
- DWI – (Driving While Impaired) not the same as "driving while intoxicated." Some states will charge you even if BAC is below .08.
- Aggravated DUI – this charge is more serious because it involves driving while under the influence of alcohol with kids in the car, with a suspended license, speeding, or your BAC comes back .15 or higher.
- Felony DUI – if this is a repeat offense or you hurt or kill someone while driving under the influence.

Places Where You Can Legally Drink on the Street

Austin, Texas permits public consumption of alcohol is legal except in six designated areas around downtown and The University of Texas, along Lady Bird Lake and Bouldin Creek, and in three East Austin neighborhoods

The Restaurant Compendium for the Curious

Butte, Montana allows open containers from 8a.m. to 2a.m. No open containers in vehicles while on a highway.

Canton, Ohio Home of the Pro Football Hall of Fame, allows carrying alcoholic drinks within the Designated Outdoor Refreshment Area (DORA), which is 69 acres of land in downtown Canton. Drinks must be in the official plastic 16-ounce cup and must be purchased from participating businesses. To go drinks are available from noon to midnight every day. Cannot drink inside vehicles.

Erie, Pennsylvania allows drinking in public parks (and other public spaces).

Fredericksburg, Texas allows drinking beer, wine, or liquor while shopping on Main Street. You cannot, however, take a mixed beverage outside where you purchased it.

Hood River, Oregon has no laws prohibiting open containers. However, it is illegal to open a beer on the premises and walk outside, but it is ok to open it *after* you step outside.

Kansas City, Missouri The entertainment district, known as the Power and Light District of Kansas City, allows open, plastic containers in public until 3am

Key West, Florida Nope, open containers of alcohol are not permitted in Key West city limits. The Key West Municipal Code **prohibits open plastic containers of alcoholic beverages in public, however**, another ordinance states that there must be one verbal or written warning for any first-time offender if compliance is achieved.

Las Vegas, Nevada allows **public drinking throughout Las Vegas, with few exceptions.** Carrying an open container of alcohol and consuming it publicly is legal in the city of Las Vegas and unincorporated Clark County, which includes the Strip. It illegal to carry glass beverage containers on the Strip. Bars are free to stay open 24 hours a day. There are some exceptions: Drinking isn't allowed within 1,000 feet of a church, synagogue, public or private school, hospital, withdrawal management facility, or homeless shelter.

Memphis, Tennessee is the only area in Tennessee where open container laws do not apply. Within the Beale Street historic district, you can carry an open container on public streets and between bars. Last call is 3am.

New Orleans, Louisiana allows anyone to carry an open container of alcohol in the French Quarter on the public streets, sidewalks, parks, or public rights-of-way as long as the container is not an opened glass container, it must be in a plastic to-go cup. Open containers of alcohol are illegal in vehicles even in New Orleans.

Savannah, Georgia permits carrying open drinks in plastic, 16-ounce cups but must remain within the Historic District.

Sonoma, California allows you to drink openly only on Sonoma Plaza from 11:30 a.m. until sunset.

States That Allow Alcohol Delivery

44 of the 50 states allow deliveries of alcohol, though specific laws differ from state to state. Three states prohibit it (Alabama, Mississippi, Utah) and three others (Kentucky, Delaware, Rhode Island) allow, but with serious restrictions and exceptions.

Most Available Expensive Liquors in the World
These are available at stores, *not* just at auction
Descriptions and prices are from their own websites

Macallan 81-year-old single malt scotch "The Reach"
$125,000
It comes from a single sherry-seasoned cask and only 288 bottles have been filled. The decanter is held up by three hands cast in bronze.

Remy Martin Black Pearl Louis XIII Anniversary Edition
$28,800 750ml
To celebrate its 140th anniversary, the House of LOUIS XIII unveiled a limited series of just 775 decanters of the LOUIS XIII Black

Pearl Anniversary Edition. These numbered decanters were drawn from a unique 572-litre tierçon, part of the family's reserve in the Domaine de Merpins.

Dalmore Single Malt 40-Year-Old
$7,999.99 750 ml

750ml. 42% ABV. This rarified bottling was initially matured in American white oak ex-Bourbon barrels and then moved to precious 30-year old Matusalem Oloroso Sherry casks. Finally, it was married with whiskies finished in Graham's Colheita Port pipes from 1970, resulting in a luscious, complex expression of The Dalmore.

The Macallan Double Cask 30 years old
$5,699 750ml

Part of the Macallan decanter series.

The Macallan No. 6
$5,024 75cl

A rich and elegant single malt scotch whisky, enticingly dark in color. 43% ABV

LOUIS XIII Cognac
$4,299 750 ml

The LOUIS XIII Classic decanter has remained the ultimate expression of our finest eaux-de-vie since 1874, an exquisite blend sourced from Grande Champagne terroir, the first cru of the Cognac region

Ichiro's Malt and Grain
$2,654 700ml

A blended whisky from the king of independent Japanese distillers, Ichiro Akuto, bottled in 2019. The nose is full of citrus and peach aromas, with wafts of vanilla in the background, while the palate offers notes of caramel and toasted oak as well

Most Expensive Period (Available at Auction)
Descriptions and prices are from their own websites

Billionaire Vodka. 6-liter Methuselah
Only $3,750,000

The vodka is triple distilled and made from natural spring water obtained from the spring supplying Caverswall Castle of England which is known to have healing properties. The vodka is first ice-filtered, then filtered through Nordic birch charcoal and finally passed through sand made from crushed diamonds and gems before being contained within the finest receptacle available on earth. It comes in a Platinum and Rhodium encased diamond encrusted crystal bottle with solid gold labels and neckband encrusted with channel set diamonds and Billionaire embellishment and crowned with a numbered diamond speckled hand mounted platinum flocked foil seal.

Tequila Ley.925,
$1,800,000

Tequila Ley is a 100% blue agave tequila with a complex aroma and flavor. It possesses an impetuous and intense character. Its clarity and nobility make it a worthy son of its Jalisco roots. When sipped, this tequila has a rounded flavor and a long finish. It is embellished on a beautiful crystalline bottle with pewter detailing that makes it shine as silver.

Bowmore 1957
$165,000

Distilled in 1957 and bottled in 2011, this marvel has been lying in wait in the finest oak casks for more than half a century. With only 12 bottles in existence, not only is this the oldest whisky we have ever released, it is also the oldest Islay single malt scotch whisky ever released.

Cicerone Beer Certification

Cicerone has become the industry standard for individuals who have attained significant knowledge and professional skills in beer sales and service of beer. It requires knowledge in keeping and serving beer, beer styles, beer flavor, evaluation, beer ingredients, brewing processes, and pairing beer with food.

Note: Cicerone is an old English word meaning a guide for visitors and sightseers to museums and galleries to explain archaeological, antiquarian, historic, or artistic subjects.

4 levels of Cicerone Certification Program

Level 1 Certified Beer Server (written examination covering the language of beer, beer service, and preserving the quality of beer.

Level 2 Certified Cicerone (written examination, tasting and demonstration parts)

Level 3 Advanced Cicerone (written exam, oral exam, and tasting assessments)

Level 4 Master Cicerone (given once per year. Two-day examination includes multiple written, oral, and tasting assessments)

Wine certifications

The Court of Master Sommeliers was established to encourage improved standards of beverage knowledge and service in hotels and restaurants. The first successful Master Sommelier examination was held in the United Kingdom in 1969. Today, The Court of Master Sommeliers had become the premier international examining body.

Introductory Sommelier (two-day tasting and theory lecture followed by a multiple-choice exam)

Certified Sommelier (one day examination consisting of theory, tasting, and service)

Advanced Sommelier (Court of Master Sommeliers recommend taking a year between the Certified Sommelier and the Advanced Sommelier programs. Two years of industry experience is required before you're eligible to take this course).

Master Sommelier (See below)

Deeper Dive
Master Sommelier

Since 1969, the total number in the world is only 273

Before being able to take the Master Sommelier exams, candidates must first take and successfully pass the Introductory, Certified, and Advanced exams. The Master Sommelier Diploma Examination consists of three parts: an oral theory examination, a deductive tasting of six wines, and a practical wine service examination.

Candidates must first pass the Master Sommelier Diploma Examination-THEORY. They then have three consecutive years to pass the remaining two parts of the examination. The candidate is required to wear professional attire and to provide all tools of the sommelier trade for the examination.

The candidate should exhibit a high standard of both technical and social skills throughout the examination and demonstrate the courtesy and charm of a Master Sommelier. It is also essential that the candidate demonstrate excellent salesmanship.

Cost to take the theory exam $995

Cost to take the tasting and practical exams $1,795

Beer troubleshooting

Symptom: Beer unusually pale, very light, and tasteless
Fault: Glass empty
Action: You need another beer

Symptom: Opposite wall covered with fluorescent lights
Fault: You have fallen over backward
Action: Have yourself leashed to bar

Symptom: Mouth contains cigarette butts
Fault: you have fallen forward
Action: Have yourself leashed to bar

Symptom: Beer tasteless, front of your shirt is wet
Fault: Mouth not open or glass applied to wrong part of face
Action: Retire to restroom, practice in mirror

Symptom: Feet cold and wet
Fault: Glass being held at incorrect angle
Action: Rotate glass so that open end points toward ceiling

Symptom: Feet warm and wet
Fault: Improper bladder control
Action: Stand next to nearest dog, complain about her house training

Symptom: Floor blurred
Fault: You are looking through bottom of empty glass
Action: Get someone to buy you another beer

Symptom: Floor moving
Fault: You are being carried out
Action: Find out if you are being taken to another bar

Symptom: Room seems unusually dark
Fault: Bar has closed
Action: Confirm home address with bartender

Highly Opinionated

Symptom: Taxi suddenly takes on colorful aspect and textures
Fault: Beer consumption has exceeded personal limitations
Action: Cover mouth

The World's Best Restaurant Names, Quotes, and Other Words

Some Creative Restaurant Names

Lox, Stock, and Bagels
Thai Me Up Restaurant and Brewery
A Salt & Battery
Like No Udder
Wild Thyme Café
Tequila Mockingbird
Life of Pie
Sconehenge
The Codfather
The Notorius P.I.G.
Mustard's Last Stand
For Heavens' Cakes
Thaitanic
Lord of the Fries
Latte Da Coffee Shop
Expresso Yourself Music Café
The Couch Tomato Café
Sufficient Grounds Café
Pita Pan
Thanks-a-Latte
Wok This Way
Juan in a Million
Side Wok Cafe

Some Creative Craft Beer Names

Chug Norris
(Oklahoma City Brewery, Oklahoma City, Oklahoma)

Your Manager is Bitch
(Beale's Brewery, Bedford, Virginia)

Czech Your Head
(Proper Brewing, Salt Lake City, Utah)

LL Cool Haze
(Litherman's, Concord, New Hampshire)

St. Patrick Hayze
(Atlanta Brewing, Atlanta, Georgia)

Welcome to Worcester
(Wormtown Brewery, Worcester, Massachusetts)

Tupac Shaporter
(Ivanhoe Park Brewing, Orlando, Florida)

Bring da Ruckus
(Fortnight Brewing, Cary, North Carolina)

Shut Up Kelly!
(Bone Up Brewing, Everett, Massachusetts)

Buzz Lightbeer
(Center Street Brewing, Wallingford, Connecticut)

Bockslider
(Martin House Brewing, Fort Worth, Texas)

Citrus Got Real
(Springdale Barrel Room, Framingham, Massachsetts)

Highly Opinionated

Fraggle Bock
(Portsmouth Brewery, Portsmouth, Ohio)

Pickleodeon
(Foolproof Brewing, Pawtucket, Rhode Island)

Turn Your Head and Coffee
(Smug Brewing, Pawtucket, Rhode Island)

Frickin Hazer beams
(Roughtail Brewing, Oklahoma City, Oklahoma)

Total Deutschebag
(Sour Not Sorry Brewing, Plymouth, Massachusetts)

You Might Be Saying it Wrong!
How to impress or at least not look clueless

How to pronounce the toughest restaurant menu words

Açaí
Ah sigh ee
Type of berry that some say has health benefits

Amuse Bouche
Ah MOOZ boosh

Arugula
Ah ROO gu la (not AIR ah GOO la)
Peppery, spicy, and slightly tart leafy green

Beignet
Ben YAY
Square shaped pieces of dough that are deep fried and sprinkled with powdered sugar

The Restaurant Compendium for the Curious

Bruschetta
Broo SKET tuh
Italian appetizer made with toasted bread, topped with tomatoes, Parmesan cheese, garlic, and fresh basil.

Caprese
Kah PRAY say
A type of salad with fresh mozzarella, tomatoes, and basil

Confit
Cone FEE
A cooking technique of preserving a meat by cooking it in its own fat

Coulis
Koo luhs
A puree of fruit or vegies used to enhance a dish

Croque Monsieur
Croak muhs YOOR
A grilled ham and cheese sandwich, usually made with Swiss or Gruyère cheese, that's dipped in beaten eggs then grilled

Endive
Ahn DEEV
Type of leaf used in salads

Espresso
Es press o (not EX press o)

Foie gras
FAW Grah
The liver of a duck or goose

Gyro
Yee roh
Greek sandwich made with meat cooked on a vertical rotisserie wrapped or stuffed in pita bread

Herb
Erb (herb without the h)
Practice saying Herb's Herbs

Hors d'oeuvres
OR Durves

Appetizers
Maître d'
May tra dee

The person in a restaurant who handles reservations plus servers and bussers

Pho
Fuh (like duh with an f)

Vietnamese soup dish consisting of broth, rice noodles, herbs, and meat

Prix Fixe
Pree Feeks

Meal with several courses but served from one price. The opposite of a la carte.

Quinoa
KEEN wah

Ragout
Ra Goo (Ra as in rag)

A thick seasoned stew of meat and veggies

Rillettes
Ruh **LETS**

Type of confit. Shredded pieces of cooked duck, goose. Or pork pounded into a paste with fat and spices that is spread on bread

Salmon
Sam uhn (silent L)

But, if you're name-dropping Salmon Rushdie, go ahead, pronounce the L

Timbale
TIM bayl
A layered sculpture of food

Turbot
TER boh
Type of fish

Restaurant Synonyms

Bistro	Coffee bar	Joint
Bodega	Coffee house	Lunchroom
Brasserie	Commisary	Outlet
Buffet	Cybercafe	Pavement cafe
Cabaret	Diner	Pizzeria
Cafe	Dining car	Pop-up
Cafeteria	Dive	Restaurant car
Caff	Drive-in	Saloon
Canteen	Eatery	Soda fountain
Carryout	Eating house	Steakhouse
Carvery	Greasy spoon	Teahouse
Cat Cafe	Grill	Tearoom
Chesanyama	Hole in the wall	Transport café
Chip vans	Inn	Truck stop
Chip wagons	Internet cafe	Trattoria

The Word 'Restaurant' Around the World

Arabic: Mateam
Catalan: Restaurant
Finnish: Ravintola
French: Restaurant
German: Gaststätte
Greek: Estiatório
Hindi: Restorent
Icelandic: Veitingahús
Irish: Bialann
Japanese: Resutoran
Korean: Leseutolang

Latin: Popina
Mandarin: Cāntīng
Māori: Wharekai
Norwegian: Restaurant
Russian: Pectopah
Spanish: Restaurante
Swedish: Restaurang
Swahili: Mgahawa
Vietnamese: Quán ăn
Welsh: Bwyty
Yiddish: Restoran

Quotes

Reminds me of my safari in Africa. Somebody forgot the corkscrew and for several days we had to live on nothing but food and water.
~ W.C. Fields

Sometimes too much to drink is barely enough.
~ Mark Twain

My grandmother is over 80 and still doesn't need glasses. Drinks right out of the bottle.
~ Henny Youngman

"Time, gentlemen, please!"
~ Called out at closing time in English pubs

Only Irish coffee provides in a single glass all four essential food groups: alcohol, caffeine, sugar, and fat.
~ Alex Levine

Every loaf of bread is a tragic story of grain that could have become beer, but didn't.

Eat, drink, and be merry, for tomorrow we may diet.

No one welcomes change except a wet baby.

The Restaurant Compendium for the Curious

24 hours in a day, 24 beers in a case. Coincidence?

There are 3 kinds of accountants—
those that can count and those that can't.

Service, not servitude.

You don't have to be crazy to work here. We'll train you.

We may live without poetry, music, and art;
We may live without conscience,
And live without heart;
We may live without friends;
We may live without books;
But civilized man cannot live without cooks.
~ Owen Meridith

If this is coffee, then bring me some tea.
If this is tea, then bring me some coffee.
~ Abraham Lincoln

No one is as cheap as the rich
~ Glenn Bernbaum (owner of Mortimer's Restaurant 1976-1998)

The bigger we are, the smaller we have to act.
~ Randy Garutti, CEO, Shake Shack

Only 3 people you need: one to get born, one to feed,
and one to bury.
A cook has the longest and most important part.

"Nobody comes to this restaurant. It's too crowded."
~ Yogi Berra

She was a good cook, as cooks go, and as cooks go, she went.
~ English author, Saki (H.H. Munro)

"It's difficult for a woman to fit in. Often the choice is to be the older sister, the younger sister, one of the boys, or the mother figure." Jana
~ Muller, Head Chef

Peter Earnest, ex-CIA spy was being interviewed. The conversation got around to James Bond liking his martini shaken, not stirred. When asked how he liked his martini, he replied,
"One after the other."

One morning as I went to the freezer, I asked my wife, "What should I take out for dinner? Without any hesitation, she replied, "Me."
~ Anonymous

The taste of the roast depends on the handshake of the host.
~ Ben Franklin

Never eat at a Chinese restaurant named
Mama Teresa's Trattoria.
~ Joy Behar

In a restaurant, the smallest hole will eventually empty the largest container unless it was made to intentionally drain,
in which case it will clog.

I started out with nothing. I still have most of it.

On Managing

If you're the boss and stop rowing,
don't be surprised if everyone else stops rowing

Remember, there are two ultimate secrets to success in business:
Number One - Never tell everything you know

Restaurants tend to say, "The answer is yes. What's the question?"
Nightclubs tend to say, "No. The answer is no."

Don't lose a good one. Don't keep a bad one.

You'll get what you **IN**spect, not what you **EX**pect.

No one appreciates what I do until I don't do it.

Bad service happens all by itself.
Good service must be managed
~ Karl Albrecht

Leadership is the art of getting someone else to do something you want done because he wants to do it.
~ Dwight D. Eisenhower

Constant, gentle pressure is my preferred technique for leadership, guidance, and coaching.
~ Danny Meyer

The rate of unemployment is 100%
if you're the one who's unemployed.

Experience may or may not be the best teacher, but it's certainly the hardest—nowhere else do you get the test first,
the lesson later.

The person who knows how, will always have a job.
The person who knows why, will always be his boss.

Only the mediocre are always at their best.
~ Jean Giraudoux

If you're not serving the guest,
you'd better be serving someone who is.

The way my boss sees it, there may not be an I in Team but there is an M and an E.

Highly Opinionated

I don't like to eat snails. I like to eat fast food.
~ Steven Wright

Understand that you cannot motivate everyone.

Managers generally get the employees they deserve.

It's better to know it and not need it,
then to need it and not know it.

If you are not fired with enthusiasm,
you will be fired with enthusiasm.
~ Vince Lombardi

Teamwork is a lot of people doing what I say.
~ The boss

At my company it's my fault if I make a mistake.
When my manager makes a mistake, it's called experience.

I'm like a menu at an expensive restaurant;
you can look at me, but you can't afford me.
~ Anna Kournikova

A leader is one who knows the way,
goes the way and shows the way
~ John C. Maxwell

A great restaurant doesn't distinguish itself by
how few mistakes it makes,
but by how well they handle those mistakes
~ Danny Meyer

Q. How did you become successful?
A. By making the right decisions.

Q. How did you know which decisions to make?
A. By the experiences I've had.

Q. How did you gain experience?
A. By making bad decisions.

Why do some people hate work, but love accomplishments?

When the game is over,
the king and the pawn go back in the same box

If you know what you're doing, go like hell.
If you're not sure, don't use your spurs.

When you don't know how to measure service, you don't.

You cut costs because you can.
~ J Self

Opportunity is missed by most people because it comes
dressed in overalls and looks like work
~ Thomas Edison

Life can only be understood backwards,
but it must be lived forwards
~ Kierkegaard

If it wasn't for the last minute; nothing would get done .

Everything should be made as simple as possible, but no simpler.
~ Albert Einstein

If you can smile when things go wrong,
you have someone in mind to blame.

It's easy to be a team when you're winning.

There's a story about a guy who never took a vacation.
When he was up for review, the human resource department

realized that he had never taken a vacation.
They called him in and asked him why.
He replied that he had never taken a vacation for two reasons:
Because the company may do worse while I'm gone.
Because the company may do better while I'm gone.

Beet ever so onion there snow peas legume.

It's not the size of the roast, it is the grip of the host
~ Ben Franklin

There was a couple who had a son who would not say anything.
The first year, not a word. Two years old, nothing.
The parents finally took him to the doctor when he was three,
but the doctor found nothing wrong. When the boy was six years old,
they were having breakfast, when the child suddenly exclaimed,
"The toast is burnt."
The mother and father were astonished and asked,
"Why haven't you said anything till now?"
The boy replied, "Up until now, everything was ok"

Original
Cogito ergo sum (I think, therefore I am)
Improved:
Cogito ergo dim sum.
(I think, therefore these are pork buns)
~ Robert Byrne

Part of the secret of success in life is to eat what you like and let the food fight it out inside.
~ Mark Twain

The trouble with jogging is the ice falls out of your glass.
~ Martin Mull

There are only two things our customers have: time and money, and they don't like spending either of them, so we better sell them their hamburgers quickly.
~ James McLamore (co-founder of Burger King)

Palindromes
(Words and sentences that spell the same frontwards or backwards)

Won ton? No Don. Not now.
Ron, I'm a minor.
Yo! Banana boy!
No lemon, no melon
Ma handed Edna ham
Spoon it in. Oops!
Stir grits
Salad, alas
Ana, nab a banana.
Boredom ala mode, Rob?
A nut for a jar of tuna
Evil olive
Feeble Tom's motel beef
Go hang a salami! I'm a lasagna hog!
Gong! Get set, Ed, to not detest eggnog.
I saw desserts. I'd no lemons, alas no melon. Distressed was I.
No cab, eh, Ted? I sat up. I put aside the bacon.
No way a papaya won!
Red rum, sir, is murder.
Sit on a potato pan, Otis
Wonton on salad? Alas, no, not now.

Restaurant Slang

2 top, 4 top, etc. – table that seats 2 or 4, etc.

86'd – A menu item has run out. ("86 the apple pie!"). Some say the term got its start when a person was escorted to Pier 86 and thrown off with a cement block tied to him. Some say it started in the soup kitchens of the Great Depression, where the standard soup pot held 85 cups of soup, so the 86th person was out of luck. Some say the term originated during the Korean war when the F-86 fighter jet shot down an enemy plane, it was 86'd. Bottom line? No one really knows where it started

All day – Total number of an item or items so the cook knows how many should be on the grill or working. "I've got 4 burgers and 5 chicken all day."

Back of the house – Employees in the kitchen, those with no customer contact, such as chefs, prep cooks, cooks, and dishwashers.

Bubble dancer – Disrespectful name for dishwasher

Campers – Customers who stay WAY too long

Cover – Customer

Double sat – Host seating the same server with 2 sets of customers at the same time.

Expo – (short for expediter), stands in front of the cook window and organizes food dishes for the servers

Front of the house – employees in front of the kitchen and with guest contact, such as the servers, bartenders, hosts and hostesses, bussers

Hockey puck – Well done steak or burger

In the weeds – Really, really busy and a server/bartender/cook is just about to lose it, like when a server gets seated twice or gets a table of 12 when she already has plenty of other tables. "Help! I'm in the weeds!"

In the window – An order ready to go to the customer

On the fly/on the rail – I need it NOW! "I need 2 fries on the rail!"

Runner – Employee who "runs" the prepared food to the servers' table

Sanitary engineer – Common term for the dishwasher

Upsell – To try to get the customer to buy a more expensive menu item. "Instead of a bourbon and coke, how about having a Single Barrel Henry McKenna and coke?"

The Restaurant Compendium for the Curious

Walk-in – The huge refrigerator that can be 'walked in' that stores all perishable meat, produce, and dairy

Walked – A customer who left without paying ("Table 4 just walked!")

Well liquor – Cheap stuff when no brand name is specified, like in a bourbon and coke. The bottles are kept in the "well" in front of the bartender. Usually bourbon, rum, scotch, vodka, tequila, and gin

HIGHLY OPINIONATED

People, People, People
Bring On the Bling!
Restaurants Owned by Celebrities

Zach Braff, Mermaid Oyster Bar, NYC, New York

Jimmy Buffett, Margaritaville, Hollywood, Florida

Sandra Bullock, Walton's Fancy and Staple, Austin, Texas.

Ty Burrell (Modern Family), The Eating Establishment, Miami, Florida

Chris Brown, Burger King locations

Francis Ford Coppola, Rustic, Francis's Favorites, Geyserville, California; Café Zoetrope, San Francisco, California; Rustic, Geyserville, California

Ayesha Curry (Basketball), International Smoke, San Francisco, California

Robert DeNiro, Locanda Verde, Manhattan, New York & Nobu Malibu, numerous locations; Tribeca Grill, NYC; Nobu, numerous locations; Locanda Verde, NYC, New York.

Drake, PICK 6IX, Toronto, Canada

Ernie Els, Ernie Els Wines Restaurant, Stellenbosch, South Africa

Eminem – Mom's Spaghetti, Detroit, Michigan and Uncasville, Connecticut

Gloria and Emilio Estefan, Estefan Kitchen, Miami

Gloria Estefan, Larios on the Beach, Miami Beach, Florida

Joey Fatone, Fat One's Hot Dogs & Italian Ice, Orlando, Florida

Florida Georgia Line, FGL House, Nashville, Tennessee

Lady Gaga, Joanne Trattoria, NYC, New York

Chip and Joanna Gaines, Magnolia Table, Waco, Texas

Richard Gere, Bedford Post Inn, Beford, New York

Ryan Gosling, Tagine Beverly Hills, Beverly Hills, California

Sammy Hagar, Cabo Wabo Cantina, numerous locations

The Restaurant Compendium for the Curious

Armie Hammer, Bird Bakery, San Antonio, Texas

Hugh Jackman, Laughing Man Coffee and Tea, NYC, New York

Jay-Z, 40/40 Club, NYC, New York

Scarlett Johansson, Yummy Pop, Paris, France

Michael Jordan, Michael Jordan's Steak House, numerous locations; 1000 North, Jupiter, Florida (co-owners: Michael Jordan, Ernie Els, Justin Thomas, Marvin Shanken)

Jon Bon Jovi, JBJ Soul Kitchen, Red Bank, New Jersey. You pay what you can afford at this non-profit community restaurant

Sebastian Junger, The Half King, NYC

Toby Keith, Toby Keith's I Love This Bar & Grill, multiple locations, Oklahoma

Ralph Lauren, Polo Bar, NYC

Giada de Laurentis, Pronto by Giada, Las Vegas

Ludacris – Ludacris's Chicken + Beer, Hartsfield-Jackson Airport, Atlanta, Georgia

Peyton Manning, Papa John's, Denver, Colorado

Moby, Moby's Little Pine, non-profit vegan restaurant in Los Angeles, California

Greg Nicotero and **Norman Reedus,** Nic & Norman's, Senoia, Georgia

Chris Noth, The Cutting Room, NYC

Shaq O'Neill, Five Guys, multiple locations

Arnold Palmer, Arnold Palmer's Restaurant, Coachella Valley, California

Robert Redford, Zoom, Park City, Utah

Susan Sarandon, SPIN New York, New York City, New York and SPIN San Francisco, San Francisco, California

Arnold Schwarzenegger, Bruce Willis, Sylvester Stallone, Planet Hollywood, numerous locations

Quentin Tarantino, Do Hwa, NYC

Highly Opinionated

Channing Tatum, Saints and Sinners, New Orleans, Louisiana

Justin Timberlake, Southern Hospitality, NYC and Colorado

Danny Trejo, Trejo's Tacos, Los Angeles, California

Lisa Vanderpump, Tom Tom, SUR, Pump and Villa Blanca, Los Angeles

Mark Wahlberg, Wahlburgers, numerous locations

Hines Ward, Table 86, Pittsburg, Pennsylvania

Pharrell Lanscilo Williams, Swan and Bar Bevy, Orlando, Florida

Venus Williams, Jamba Juice locations

Vince Young, Vince Young Steakhouse, Austin, Texas

Celebrity Restaurants That Didn't Make It

Britney Spears' Nyla (abbreviation for New York and Louisiana), Manhattan, New York (2002-2002)

The Fashion Café by Naomi Campbell, Elle Macpherson, Claudia Schiffer, and Christy Turlington (1995-1998)

J. Lo's Madre's. Pasadena, California. (2002-2008)

Steven Spielberg's Dive! Los Angeles, California (1994 – 1999)

Eva Longoria's Beso's, Las Vegas, Nevada (2008-2012)

Eva Longoria's She by Morton's, Las Vegas, Nevada (2012-2014)

The Baldwin's brothers Alaia, renamed Luahn, renamed Society 5. NYC, New York (1999-2000)

Jessica Biel's Au Fudge, Hollywood, California. (2016–2018)

Patrick Swayze's Mulholland Drive Café, New York (1988-1996)

Flavor Flav's flava-Flav's Fried Chicken, Clinton, Iowa 2011-2012). House of Flavor (2012-2012), Flavor Flav's Chicken & Ribs, Sterling Heights, Michigan (2012-2013), Flavor Flav's Chicken & Vinny's Pizza, Las Vegas, NV. (2018-2018)

Hulk Hogan's Pastamania, Bloomington, Minnesota (1995-1996)

Celebrity Chef Restaurants That Didn't Make It

Celebrity chef, Anne Burrell, (Host of Worst Cooks in America), opened 'Phil and Anne's Good Time Lounge' in Brooklyn, NY. (2017-2018)

Celebrity chef, Jonathan Waxman, (Multiple restaurant owner and guest judge on Master Chef) host for opened "Waxman's + J Bird" in San Francisco, California. (2017).

Celebrity chef, Tyler Florence, (The Great Food Truck Race and Food Court Wars and America's Best Cook) opened "Rotisserie & Wine" in Napa, California. It lasted one year.

Celebrity chef, Masaharu Morimoto, (Iron Chef), opened "Tribeca Canvas + Bisuturo" in NYC. (2013)

Celebrity chef, Jose Garces, (Iron Chef) opened "Amada NYC" in New York city, NY. (2016-2018)

Celebrity chef, Gordon Ramsay, (At least 6,000+ TV shows and multiple restaurant owner) opened "Fat Cow" in Los Angeles, California. (2012-2014)

Celebrity chef, Cat Cora, (Iron Chef), opened "Fatbird" in New York City, NY. (2016-2017)

Celebrity chef, Jamie Oliver (The Naked Chef), opened "Barbecoa Piccadilly" in London, UK. (2018)

Athlete Owned Restaurants

8-Twelve MVP Bar & Grill, Aaron Rodgers and Ryan Braun, Brookfield, Wisconsin

Arnold Palmer's Restaurant, Arnold Palmer (Golf), La Quinta, California

Baumhower's Victory Grille, Dauphin's, Bob Baumhower (Football), many locations

Billy Sims Barbecue, Billy Sims (Football), many locations

Brett Favre's Steakhouse, Brett Favre (Football) Gulfport, Mississippi

Highly Opinionated

Bubba's Q, Al "Bubba" Baker (Football), Avon, Ohio

Clyde Frazier's Wine & Dine, Walt Frazier (Basketball), NYC, New York

Ditka's, Mike Ditka (Football), Numerous locations

Elway's, John Elway (Football), Denver, Colorado

Greg Norman's Australian Grille, Greg Norman (Golf), Myrtle Beach, South Carolina

Joe DiMaggio's Restaurant, Joe DiMaggio (Baseball), San Francisco, California

Joe Theismann's, Joe Theismann (Football), Alexandria, Virginia

The Kingfish Café, Gary Payton (Basketball), Seattle, Washington

Michael Jordan's Steakhouse, numerous locations, Michael Jordan (Basketball)

Randy White's BBQ, Randy White (Football), Frisco, Texas

Tresca, Ray Bourque (Hockey), Boston, Massachusetts

Vince Young (football), Vince Young's Steakhouse, Austin, Texas

Wayne Gretzky's Restaurant, Wayne Gretzky (Hockey), Toronto, Canada

Yao Restaurant & Bar, Yao Ming (Basketball) Houston, Texas

Athlete Owned Restaurants That Didn't Make It

Big Papi's Grille, David Ortiz (Baseball)

Center Court with C-Webb, Chris Webber (Basketball), Sacramento, California

Cheli's Pub and Grill, Chris Chelios (Hockey), Aurora, Illinois

Pujols 5 Grill, Albert Pujols (Baseball), St. Louis, Missouri

Giants of the Industry

Norman Brinker (1931 – 2009)

His restaurant career began with Jack in the Box in 1957 when it had only five locations and was later named president with an equity interest. After Jack in the Box went public, Brinker left the company, moved to Dallas, Texas and bought a coffee shop that he renamed Brinks. In 1966, he started Steak & Ale Restaurants that grew into a chain of 109 restaurants. Steak & Ale was the very beginning of casual dining, where customers could get a full service, sit-down meal at a moderate price. Steak and Ale was also one of the first to start the all-you-can-eat salad bar.

But one innovation that maybe should have been left un-innovated was the ubiquitous greeting "Hi, my name is Billy, and I'll be your waiter tonight."

Brinker sold Steak & Ale to Pillsbury in 1976 and was named head of the restaurant division where he helped develop the Bennigan's chain of restaurants. In 1983, he left Pillsbury to purchase the controlling interest in Chili's, a chain of 23 restaurants in Dallas and Houston.

Brinker expanded Chili's and took it public in 1984 (EAT). In 1991, the corporate name was changed from Chili's to Brinker International when it added more restaurant brands than just Chili's.

By 1995, Brinker International had more than 1,400 restaurants worldwide, 90,000 employees, and more than $3 billion in sales. Today, Brinker International includes Chili's Grill and Bar, Maggiano's Little Italy, and two virtual brands, 'It's Just Wings' and 'Maggiano's Italian Classics' which operate out of existing Chili's and Maggiano's Little Italy restaurants. In 2021, Brinker International did over 3.34 billion dollars.

In 1993, Brinker was seriously injured during a polo match when he was crushed by his horse. He was in a coma for three weeks, paralyzed for three months, but back at work within four months.

An amazing fact is the incredible number of restaurant leaders that started at Steak and Ale. A display at the University of Houston's Hilton School of Hotel and Restaurant Management lists 53 restaurant chains whose origins trace back to Brinker.

In 1952, he was on the U.S. Olympic equestrian team and later competed in the 1954 Modern Pentathlon World Championships in Budapest, Hungary. He helped his third wife, Nancy Goodman, establish the Susan G. Komen for the Cure Charity, in the name of his wife's sister who died of breast cancer.

Marie-Antoine Carême (1783–1833)

He was possibly the first celebrity chef. He was named for Marie Antoinette, but he preferred to be called "Antonin."

He is known as the founder of "La Grande Cuisine Française." This cuisine is known for being excessive and overformal, typically with Victorian opulence, and often associated with royal courts. So, basically simple, understated, and humble food and service for the common folk. Not.

He classified French sauces into four mother sauces (Velouté, Béchamel, Allemande, and Espagnole) that are still known today.

He instituted the white double-breasted kitchen jackets and toques (the tall white hats with folded pleats). He required the hats and coats be white because white is associated with cleanliness.

Carême was born in Paris to a poor family which had between 15 and 25 children. He was sent off somewhere between 8 and 12 years old. A tavern keeper gave him a 6-year apprenticeship, starting as a potwasher. At the age of 17, Carême began an apprenticeship with Sylvain Bailly, a famous Parisian pastry chef, and was encouraged to learn to read and write. Later, he became known for reproducing famous architectural works in sugar and pastry that he had seen in books. In 1815, Carême went to London to work as head chef for George, Prince of Wales, who would become King George IV of England in 1820.

He wrote several influential books:
- (date unknown) Le Maitre d'Hôtel Français
- 1815 Le Pâtissier Royal Parisien, ou traité élémentaire et pratique de la Pâtisserie ancienne et moderne de l'Entremets de sucre, des entrées froides et des socles
- (date unknown) Le Pâtissier Pittoresque
- 1828 Le Cuisinier Parisienne
- 1833 L'Art de la Cuisine Française au dix-neuvième siècle

Buwei Yang Chao (1889-1981)

She was born in China and studied medicine in Japan to become a medical doctor. After that, she returned to China as one of the first female physicians to practice western medicine in China. She married Yuen Ren Chao (1892-1982), a linguist, and moved to Cambridge, Massachusetts in 1938 where he was a trainer and translator at Harvard University, teaching Mandarin.

In 1945, her husband, Yuen Ren Chao, and daughter, Rulan, collaborated in the translation of the cookbook, coined the terms "pot sticker" and "stir fry" for her English language cookbook, 'How to Cook and Eat in Chinese'.

From the original 1945 edition:

"…a big-fire-shallow-fat-continual-stirring-quick-frying of cut-up material with wet seasoning. So, we shall call it stir fry."

These words were coined because there were no English equivalent words. The book was first published in 1945, with subsequent editions in 1948, 1956, 1963, and 1972. Pearl S. Buck, author of the Pulitzer Prize winning "The Good Earth," wrote the book's preface.

Samuel (1867-1925) and William (1865-1938) Childs

They founded the Childs Restaurant chain in 1889. They were the first to employ female servers, invented the cafeteria tray line format in 1898, and in 1919, began an employee stock ownership plan for its restaurant managers and later, its employees. Within 10 years, employees owned almost 25% of the company's common stock. At its peak in 1925, the company had 107 locations in 33 cities, serving 50 million meals annually, with a profit of $2 million each year, which in 2022 dollars is $34 million.

Josephine Cochrane (1839-1913)

As a socialite, Cochrane hated when her fine China would chip after hand washing. In 1886, she decided to invent something that would eliminate hand washing. She made wire racks to keep the dishes in place, set into a wooden wheel which was inside of a copper boiler filled with hot water. With a crank or small motor, the wheel turned, splashing hot water onto the dishes. After getting a patent in 1886, she went into production and showed her Cochrane dishwasher at the 1893 World's Columbian Exposition in Chicago, which won the highest prize for her design's durability, adaptability, and mechanical construction. In 1916, her company was bought out by Hobart, which became KitchenAid, which is now Whirlpool Corporation. She was posthumously inducted into the National Inventors Hall of Fame in 2006 for her invention of the dishwasher.

Bill Darden (1919–1994).

He started out with the Green Frog (Service with a hop), a 25-seat luncheonette in Waycross, Georgia when he was 19 years old. Of note is that he did not segregate the Green Frog. Recognizing that Florida was becoming wildly popular, he invested in Howard Johnson's hotels and restaurants in Florida. He opened the first Red Lobster in 1968 in Lakeland, Florida. By 1970, there were 5 Red Lobsters which got the attention of General Mills. They bought the concept and made Darden an executive. Later, when they opened Olive Garden, they named the division Darden Restaurants.

Today, Darden's restaurants include Olive Garden, LongHorn Steakhouse, Cheddar's Scratch Kitchen, Yard House, The Capital Grille, Seasons 52, Bahama Breeze and Eddie V's totaling over 1,850 restaurants with 180,000 employees, making Darden one of the 50 largest private employers in America and serving more than 400 million guests annually in North America.

Auguste Escoffier (1846-1935)

How does a chef get into a book about restaurants? Simple. Because he had such an incredible influence on restaurants. Escoffier modernized menus, reduced the number of courses served at a formal meal, influenced the art and practice of cooking, and revolutionized the organization of the professional kitchen. Three of his cookbooks are still regarded as indispensable. He was known as "Le Roi des Chefs et le Chef des Rois" ("The King of Chefs and the Chef of Kings").

He spent 7 years in the army as a chef and later as chef de cuisine of the Rhine Army. He opened his first restaurant, Le Faisan d'Or (The Golden Pheasant) in Cannes, France. He wrote Le Guide Culinaire in 1903 and Ma Cuisine in 1934.

He organized programs to help feed the hungry and financially assist retired chefs. Escoffier was recognized by the French Government when he was made him a Chevalier of the Legion d'Honneur in 1920 and an Officer in 1928.

Fred Harvey (1835–1901)

Known for creating the first restaurant chain in the United States. In 1976, he opened restaurants, called "Harvey Houses" along the Atchison, Topeka, and Santa Fe Railroad in the Southwest. He increased sales by starting the "Harvey Girl." These were all young women who were hired as waitresses. They were provided housing, had to follow strict rules, and not permitted to marry until they had worked at least a year. Because of the 5,000 Harvey Girls hired, he influenced the civilizing of the southwest.

There were 84 Harvey Houses at its peak. Some say his last words were "Don't cut the ham too thick, boys." While others say his last words were "Cut the ham thinner, boys."

Howard Johnson (1897 – 1972)

He began with a soda shop in Quincy, Massachusetts in 1925 and added a second in 1929. In 1935, he created one of the first restaurant franchises.

Howard Johnson's legacy includes creating one of the first restaurant franchises, centralized buying and commissaries that prepared food for the restaurants; all meant to ensure uniform consistency, quality, and lower costs. After World War II, Johnson created the motel (motor hotel). By 1965, there were 770 restaurants and 265 motels along major roads in the US.

Ray Kroc (1902–1984)

After a series of jobs, Kroc became the distributor of a type of blender that could mix up to five milk shakes at a time. In 1954, he visited McDonald Brothers restaurant which were using 8 mixers, and the rest is history. First, he became the franchising agent for the brothers in 1955. Then, later, in 1961, he bought the McDonald brother's restaurants for $2.7 million.

One of Kroc's major contributions to the success of McDonald's was the strict rules for standardization that made sure all McDonald's food was the same everywhere.

Kroc was president of McDonald's, Chairman of the Board, and Senior Chairman of the Board in 1977. Also, in 1977, he published his autobiography, "Grinding it out: The Making of McDonald's."

He owned the San Diego Padres major League baseball team.

Maurice (1902-1971) and Richard (1909-1998) McDonald

The brothers first bought the 750-seat Mission Theater 20 miles outside of Los Angeles. They put in a snack bar and renamed it the Beacon. After seven years, the McDonald brothers sold their movie.

In 1941, the McDonald's brothers opened McDonald's BBQ. After 8 years, they made the very gutsy decision to close for several months to take a hard look at their operation. They had started out with 25 menu items with BBQ as the main item. After focusing on the menu, labor, and speed, they eliminated BBQ and went to a menu of only three items: burgers, shakes, and fries. They eliminated car hops in favor of counter service. This by itself was risky, since they were forcing their customers to get out of their cars to get served. At the same time, they introduced their version of the assembly line with what they called "Speedy Service System." With those changes, they completely revolutionized the fast-food industry.

Richard Melman (1942-)

Founder and chairman of Lettuce Entertain You Enterprises (LEYE) which has opened more than 150 restaurants across 11 states. In 1971, he and his partner, Jerry Orzoff, opened his first restaurant, RJ Grunts. According to the Lettuce Entertain You website, Melman had a philosophy based on the importance of partnership, sharing responsibilities and ideas, developing and growing together, with a "culture of caring."

Danny Meyer (1958-)

1985, when he was 27 years old, he opened his first restaurant, Union Square Café. Thirty years later, the Union Square Hospitality Group (USHG) included Gramercy Tavern, The Modern, Maialino, and others. Danny and USHG founded Shake Shack, which became a public company in 2015. USHG is known for its culture of Enlightened Hospitality, the guiding principle of prioritizing employees first. In 2006, he wrote the New York Times bestseller, "Setting the Table" (HarperCollins).

He received the 2017 Julia Child Award, the 2015 TIME 100 "Most Influential People" list, the 2012 Aspen Institute Preston Robert

Tisch Award in Civic Leadership, the 2011 NYU Lewis Rudin Award for Exemplary Service to New York City, and the 2000 IFMA Gold Plate Award. USHG's restaurants and individuals have won 28 James Beard Awards, including Outstanding Restaurateur (2005) and Who's Who of Food and Beverage in America (1996).

Wolfgang Puck (1949-)

In 1982, he opened his first restaurant, Spago in Los Angeles. Later, he started the Wolfgang Puck Companies (Fine Dining Group, Wolfgang Puck Catering, and Wolfgang Puck Worldwide). These include over 20 fine dining restaurants, bars and lounges, and airport and Gelson's locations.

In 1993, Spago Hollywood was inducted into the Nation's Restaurant News Fine Dining Hall of Fame and The James Beard Restaurant of the Year Award. In 2002, Puck received the 2001–2002 Daytime Emmy Award for Outstanding Service Show, *Wolfgang Puck*.

Spago Beverly Hills received a James Beard Foundation Outstanding Service Award in 2005. It was awarded two Michelin stars in the 2008 and 2009 Los Angeles Michelin Guide.

CUT Beverly Hills was awarded a Michelin star in 2007. In 2013, Puck was inducted into the Culinary Hall of Fame. In July 2016, CUT at the Marina Bay Sands, Singapore was awarded a Michelin Star. On April 26, 2017, he received a star on the Hollywood Walk of Fame, for his work in the TV industry. On May 20, 2017, he was named the International Foodservice Manufacturers Association (IFMA) 2017 Gold Plate Winner.

Harland Sanders (1890-1980)

In 1930, at the age of 40, Sanders ran a service station in Corbin, Kentucky when he began serving meals, but fried chicken was not on the menu because it took too long to prepare, but that changed in 1939 when he switched to pressure cookers.

Sanders was 65 when Pete Harman became the first franchisee in Salt Lake City, Utah in 1952. He incorporated KFC and began adding franchisees throughout the country by going to restaurants and giving demonstrations on cooking chicken. His franchisees paid him 5 cents for every chicken sold. In 1964, the company had more than 600 franchise locations. He sold the company for $2 million to a group of investors. Sanders became the KFC spokesman and visited KFC restaurants around the world. He died at the age of 90, in Louisville, Kentucky.

Howard Schultz (1953-)

In 1982 he joined a company which sold only coffee beans, leaf teas, and spices, called Starbucks as their director of retail operations and marketing. In 1985, he quit Starbucks when he could not convince the owners to sell espresso drinks. In 1986, he and investors opened a coffee shop called "Il Giornale." In 1987, he bought Starbucks and after a couple of years, renamed Il Giornale to Starbucks and started to grow. He is credited with introducing espresso drinks to the United States and creating "coffee culture." In 1992, he took Starbucks public (SBUX). By the time of his retirement, in 2018, Starbucks had grown to over 28,000 locations in 77 countries.

In 2014, Schultz launched the Starbucks College Achievement Plan, a partnership with Arizona State University, which allows all employees at Starbucks working 20 or more hours a week to qualify for free tuition through ASU's online courses.

In 1997, he wrote "Pour Your Heart into it: How Starbucks Built a Company One Cup at a Time" with Dori Jones Yang; In 2011, he wrote "Onward: How Starbucks fought for its life without losing its soul" with Joanne Gordon. In 2014, he wrote "For Love of Country: What Our Veterans Can Teach Us About Citizenship, Heroism, and Sacrifice" with Rajiv Chandrasekaran. In 2019, he wrote "From the Ground Up: A Journey to Reimagine the Promise of America."

During the 2000's, he owned the NBA team Seattle SuperSonics and the WNBA team Seattle Storm.

He was named Fortune Magazine's 2011 "Businessperson of the Year" and "Most Generous CEO of 2015," for the healthcare, educational opportunities, and employee stock options at Starbucks. He and Sheri Schultz co-founded the Schultz Family Foundation, supporting 'Onward Youth', which promotes employment for young people who are not in school and not working and 'Onward Veterans', helping veterans to successfully transition to civilian life.

Alice Waters (1944-)

Alice Waters opened Chez Panisse in 1971 with $10,000 in a former plumbing supply store in Berkeley, California. She was a UC Berkeley student with a French cultural studies major and Montessori teacher. Her philosophy to use the finest, freshest quality ingredients and prepare them simply without sauces caused Chez Panisse to be known as the birthplace of modern California cuisine and started a movement for restaurants to use fresh, local ingredients. Chez Panisse is named after a character in a film trilogy by Marcel Pagnol (French novelist, playwright, filmmaker).

Elena Zelayeta (1898-1974)

She was the first Mexican American with a televised cooking show, "It's Fun to Eat with Elena," televised in California.

She is the author of bestselling cookbooks, including "Elena's Secrets of Mexican Cooking" in 1968 and "Elena's Famous Mexican and Spanish Recipes," published by Prentice-Hall. Both are still available.

She was born in Mexico and learned to cook as a young girl. Her family moved to California just as she went blind at age 11. To avoid depression, she turned to cooking. Elena became an authority on cooking, gave cooking lessons to the blind, and gave talks to women's clubs. She lived in California for over fifty years.

The importance of one person

Xvxn though my typxwritxr is an old, it works vxry wxll, xxcxpt for onx kxy. You would think that with all thx othxr kxys working wxll, onx kxy would not bx noticxd or makx a diffxrxnce.

You may say to yoursxlf, wxll, I'm only onx pxrson. No onx will noticx if I don't do my bxst. But it doxs makx a diffxrxncx bxcausx to bx effxctivx, a hotxl or rxstaurant nxxds activx participation by xvxryonx.

So, thx nxxt timx you think you arx not important, rxmxmbxr my old typxwritxr. You arx a kxy pxrson.

HIGHLY OPINIONATED

How To Understand a Want Ad:

Competitive salary: We remain competitive by paying less than our competitors.

Join our fast-paced company: We have no time to train you; you'll have to introduce yourself to your co-workers.

Nationally recognized leader: Some magazine, somewhere, wrote us up a few years ago, but we haven't done anything innovative since.

Immediate opening: The person who used to have this job gave notice a month ago. We're just now running the ad.

Sales position requiring motivated self-starter: We're not going to supply you with leads; there's no base salary; you'll wait 30 days for your first commission check.

Self-motivated: Management won't answer questions.

We offer great benefits: After 90 days, you can join our HMO, which has a $1,500 deductible and a $50 co-pay.

Pension/retirement benefits: After 3 years, we'll allow you to fund your own 401(k) and, if you behave, we'll give you a 2 percent matching contribution.

Seeking enthusiastic, fun, hardworking people: who still live with their parents and won't mind our internship-level salaries.

Casual work atmosphere: We don't pay enough to expect that you'll dress up.

Competitive environment: We have a lot of turnover.

Exciting and professional work environment: Guys in gray suits will bore you with tales of squash and their weekends on yachts.

Join our dynamic team: We all listen to motivational tapes.

Fun work environment: Your co-workers will be insulted if you don't drink with them.

The Restaurant Compendium for the Curious

A drug-free work environment: We booze it up at company parties.

Must be deadline oriented: You'll be six months behind schedule on your first day.

Some public relations required: If we're in trouble, you'll go on TV and get us out of it.

Some overtime required: Some time each night and some time each weekend.

Salary range $24k-$42k: We'll always offer you $24k to start.

A highly visible position: You'll give boring speeches on your own time.

Flexible hours: Work 40 hours; get paid for 25.

Duties will vary: Anyone in the office can boss you around.

Where employees feel valued: Those who missed the last round of layoffs, that is.

Must have an eye for detail: We have no quality control.

College degree preferred: Unless you don't. Then it is ok.

Career minded: Female applicants must be childless (and remain that way).

Apply in person: If you're old, fat, or ugly you'll be told the position has been filled.

No phone calls please: We've filled the job; our call for resumes is just a legal formality.

Seeking candidates with a wide variety of experience: You'll need it to replace three people who just left.

Problem solving skills a must: You're walking into a company in perpetual chaos.

Requires team leadership skills: You'll have the responsibilities of a manager, without the pay or respect.

Good communications skills: Management communicates, you listen, figure out what they want, and do.

Ability to handle a heavy workload: You whine, you're fired.

Aspirations for growth within our company: We love brown-nosers.

How To Understand a Resume

I know how to deal with stressful situations: I'm usually on Prozac. When I'm not, I take lots of cigarette and coffee breaks.

I seek a job that will draw upon my strong communications and organizational skills: I talk too much and like to tell other people what to do.

I'm extremely adept at all manner of office organization: I've used Microsoft Office.

I'm honest, hard-working, and dependable: I pilfer office supplies.

My pertinent work experience: I hope you don't ask me about all the baby-sitting jobs I've had.

I take pride in my work: I blame others for my mistakes.

I'm balanced and centered: I'll keep crystals at my desk and do Tai Chi in the lunchroom.

I have a sense of humor: I know a lot of corny, old jokes and I tell them badly. Often.

I'm personable: I give lots of unsolicited personal advice to co-workers.

I'm willing to relocate: As I leave San Quentin, any where's better.

I'm extremely professional: I have a calendar on my phone.

My background and skills match your requirements: You're probably looking for someone more experienced.

I am adaptable: I've changed jobs a lot.

I am on the go: I'm never at my desk.

I'm highly motivated to succeed: The minute I find a better job, I'm outta there.

I have formal training: I'm a college drop-out.

I interact well with co-workers: I mean besides the sexual harassment.

Thank you for your time and consideration: Wait! Don't throw me away!

I look forward to hearing from you soon: Like, I'm gonna hold my breath waiting for your stupid form letter thanking me "for my interest and wishing me luck in my future career."

Seen On Management Resumes:

- Reason for leaving last job: Maturity leave
- Instrumental in ruining entire operation
- Company made me a scapegoat, just like my last three employers
- Received a plague for Manager of the Year

Chapter V

INSIDE
RESTAURANTS

CHEF UNIFORM

From the August Escoffier School of Culinary Arts

Chef hat (toque) (pronounced Toke)
Auguste Escoffier was a famous chef in some of Europe's most famous hotels. He had also served in the military, and he had seen that the officer with the highest plumes commanded the highest respect. So, he took the common soft chef hat, stiffened and raised the hat to a military height of 18 inches with 100 tightly ironed pleats.

The toque was introduced in 1793 ('toque blanche' translates to 'white hat'). The height of the hat can mean how experienced the chef is, but a more practical reason for the height is that the chef is visible anywhere in the kitchen. It is said that the number of pleats in the hat is the number of cooking techniques that a master chef must know. (100 pleats = 100 ways to make sauce or to cook eggs). A more reality-based reason is that the 100 starched pleats strengthened the toque's tall structure.

Chef's double-breasted coat
The coat is made of a heavy material to help protect from heat, steam, and splashing liquids while cooking. Traditionally, the coat had long sleeves to cover the arms when reaching into ovens. However, today, most uniforms are made with short sleeves for ease of movement. The coat was designed to hide stains and because the double-breasted jacket is reversible, the stains can be hidden by folding down the flaps over stains.

Chef's pants
A chef's uniform usually includes black and white houndstooth patterned pants because it hides stains and spills. They are made of lightweight and breathable material, with the waist typically elastic

or a drawstring with side and back pockets.

Chef's apron

Chefs wear an apron around their waists to protect their legs from hot spills, especially while carrying a plate or hot pot from the stove. These aprons usually end just below the knee, so the chef can quickly move around the kitchen without getting tangled in the fabric. Typically, aprons are white, black, or striped.

THE CHAINS

Restaurant Chains Open 365, 24/7
Why do they have locks on the front doors?

McDonald's (not all)
Waffle House
Whataburger

Restaurant Chains Open 365ish, 24/7ish

Boston Market (10:30 – 10pm)
Burger King (5:30 – midnight)
Denny's (6am – midnight)
Dunkin' (4am – 10pm)
IHOP (6am – 10pm)
Jack in the Box (6am – 11pm & 6am - midnight)
McDonalds (6am -10pm, 4am – 3am, others)
Perkins Restaurant & Bakery (6am – midnight, 5am – midnight, 5:30- 10pm, others)
Steak 'n Shake (10am -10pm, 11am – 7pm, 12pm – 7pm)
Taco Cabana (6am – 10pm)
White Castle (noon – midnight, 7am – 11pm, others)

Chains That Started in Each State

ALABAMA
Jack's Restaurants founded by Jack Caddell in 1960.

Bob Baumhower's Victory Grill founded by Bob Baumhower in 1981.

Checkers, started in Mobile in 1986

ALASKA
Great Alaska Pizza Company in 2003 by Mark Sines

ARIZONA
Lucky Wishbone founded in 1953 by Derald Fulton.

Cold Stone Creamery, Tempe in 1988

ARKANSAS
Slim Chickens. Founded in 2003 by Greg Smart and Tom Gordon.

CALIFORNIA
The Habit Burger Grill in 1969

In-N-Out Burger started in Baldwin Park in 1948

COLORADO
Garbanzo started in 2007

Chipotle started in 1993

CONNECTICUT
Duchess started in Bridgeport in 1956

Subway started in Bridgeport in 1965

DELAWARE
Casapulla's Subs started in 1956

Wings to Go opened in 1985

FLORIDA
PDQ started in Tampa in 2011

Burger King in 1954

GEORGIA
Waffle House started in 1955

Chick-fil-A in 1946

HAWAII
Zippy's opened in 1966

IDAHO
Moxie Java opened in 1988 in Boise

ILLINOIS
Harold's Chicken Shack started in Chicago in 1950

McDonald's (Ray Kroc) in 1955

Steak 'n Shake started in Normal in 1934

INDIANA
Schoop's Hamburgers started in Hammond in 1984

Steak 'n Shake headquarters is in Indianapolis

IOWA
Happy Joe's Pizza & Ice Cream started in Bettendorf in 1972

Maid-Rite started in 1926 in Muscatine in 1926

KANSAS
Freddy's Frozen Custard & Steakburgers started in Wichita in 2002

Pizza Hut started in 1958 by Dan and Frank Carney

KENTUCKY
Fazoli's started in Lexington in 1988

KFC in 1930

LOUISIANA
Danny & Clyde's started in Gretna in 1973

Popeyes started in New Orleans in 1972

MAINE
Luke's Lobster started in 2009

Gifford's Famous Ice Cream started in the 1800's, moved to Main in 1973

MARYLAND
Gino's Burgers & Chicken started in Baltimore in 1957

Jerry's Subs and Pizza started in 1954

MASSACHUSETTS
Tasty Burger started in Boston in 2010

Dunkin' Donuts opened in Quincy in 1950

MICHIGAN
Big John's Steak & Onion started in Flint in 1963

Comino's started in Ypsilant in 1960

MINNESOTA
MyBurger

Dairy Queen started in 1938

MISSISSIPPI
Ward's started in Hattiesburg in 1978

MISSOURI
Winstead's started in Kansas City in 1936

Panera Bread started in 1987 as Saint Louis Bread Company.

MONTANA
The Pickle Barrel started in Bozeman in 1975

Ted's Montana Grill started in Columbus in 2002

NEBRASKA
Runza started in Lincoln in 1949

Godfather's Pizza started in Omaha in 1973

NEVADA
PT's Pub opened in Las Vegas in (Tom and Phil Boeckle in 1982)

NEW HAMPSHIRE
Moe's Italian Sandwiches started in 1959

NEW JERSEY
Jersey Mike's started in Point Pleasant in 1956

Blimpie started in Hoboken in 1954

NEW MEXICO
Blake's Lotaburger opened in Alburquerque in 1952 (Blake Chanslor)

NEW YORK
Golden Krust

Sbarro opened in 1956

NORTH CAROLINA
Char-Grill

Bojangles opened in Charlotte in 1977

NORTH DAKOTA
Space Aliens Grill & Bar opened in 1997

OHIO
Skyline Chili

Wendy's opened in Columbus in 1969

OKLAHOMA
Burger Street

Sonic Drive-In opened in 1953

OREGON
Taco Time

Papa Murphy's opened in 1995

PENNSYLVANIA
Wawa opened in Folsom in 1964

Auntie Anne's started in 1988

RHODE ISLAND
Del's Lemonade started in 1948

SOUTH CAROLINA
Rush's started in St. Andrews in 1940

Denny's started in 1953

SOUTH DAKOTA
The Millstone started in 1981

TENNESSEE
Krystal started in Chatanooga in 1932

Pal's Sudden Service started in Kingsport in 1956

TEXAS
Whataburger started in Corpus Christ in 1950

UTAH
Iceberg Drive Inn started in Salt Lake City in 1960

Artic Circle started in 1924

VERMONT
Ben & Jerry's started in 1978

VIRGINIA
Five Guys started in 1986

WASHINGTON
Burgerville started in Vancouver in 1961

Starbucks started in Seattle in 1971

WEST VIRGINIA
Gino's Pizza & Spaghetti House started in 1961

WISCONSIN
Culver's started in Sauk City in 1981

WYOMING
Taco John's started in 1968

Restaurant Chains That Have Had Last Call Goodbye, RIP, Adios, Auf Wiedersehen

All-Star Café (1995-2007) Owned by Andre Agassi, Wayne Gretzky, Shaquille O'Neal, and Tiger Woods.

Arthur Treacher's – (1969-) 826 units at peak with 7 still open

Beefsteak Charlie's (Originally opened in 1910–1960's) Opened as a chain (unrelated to the original) in 1976, closed 1992 as a chain). Over 60 locations at peak.

Boston Sea Party (1976–1998) Unknown number at peak

Bresler's Ice Cream (1927–2007 when it was rebranded)

Britling Cafeterias (circa 1930-1970's) Claim to fame – Elvis Presley's mother worked there.

Bugaboo Creek Steakhouse 1992 – 2016 30 locations at peak

Burger Chef, (1957-1982). At its peak had around 1,100 locations. Many sold to Hardee's.

Burger Queen -See Druthers

Bennigan's – (1976-2008) 200 at peak. Sold to Metromedia Restaurant Group. MRG filed for bankruptcy in 2008.

Chi-Chi's, (1975-2004) over 237 locations at peak.

Chicken George (1979-1991) At its peak, had 9 company stores, unknown franchises

China Coast (1990-1995) Peak of 52 restaurants.

Clifton's Cafeteria (1931–2018). 10 locations at peak

D'Lites (1978-1987) peaked at over 100 restaurants in 1985

Doggie Diner (1948–1986). 30 locations at its peak.

The Restaurant Compendium for the Curious

Don Pablo's (1985–2019). 120 locations at peak.

Druthers, originally Burger Queen from 1956 until 1981. Had 171 locations. In 1990, converted to Dairy Queen.

ESPN Zone – started in 1998 and grew to 9 locations. One location still open at the Disneyland Resort in Anaheim, California.

Farrell's Ice Cream Parlour – (1963–2019) 130 at peak.

Fresh Choice, AKA Fresh Plus, Fresh Choice Express, Zoopa. (1986–2012)

G.D. Ritzy's – about 100. 1980. A few left today.

Gino's Burgers, (1957-1982). Most sold to Marriott in 1982, the rest converted to Roy Rogers or closed. 359 at peak.

Horn & Hardart (1902–1991)

Hot Shoppes - (1927–1999) by JW Marriott. 70 at peak.

JB's Restaurants (1961–2019) 104 restaurants at peak. 2 still open.

Kenny Rogers Roasters, (1991-1998). At peak it had 425 locations.

La Petite Boulangerie (1977–2000). 140 locations at its peak

Little Tavern (1927-2008) about 50 locations at peak

Lone Star Steakhouse 1(989–2017). 267 locations at its peak.

Lum's, (1956–1982). 450 at peak

Lyon's (1952-2012) Started by Lyons Magnus. 65 locations at its peak. Some have reopened.

Mighty Casey's (1980–1994). Most converted to Krystals.

Morrison's Cafeteria Opened in 1920, sold to Piccadilly Cafeterias in 1998. One Morrison's Cafeteria is still open in Mobile, Alabama. 151 locations at its peak

Mr. Steak (1962–2009). 258 locations at its peak

Inside Restaurants

Naugles – (1970-1995). 225 at peak. Sold to Collins Food International who merged with Del Taco in 1988. Launched comeback in 2015 and now has 3 locations.

Official All-Star Café – Backed by Shaquille O'Neal, Wayne Gretzky, Joe Montana, Monica Seles, Ken Griffey, Jr, and Andre Agassi. Owned by Planet Hollywood. (1995- 1998).

People's Restaurants. One left in Corpus Christi, Texas

Pioneer Chicken – (1961–1988) 300 at peak.

Pizza Haven (1958–1998).

Pup 'n' Taco, (1956-1984). At its peak had more than 100 locations. Sold to Taco Bell.

Pumper Nic, later just Pumper (Argentina) (1974-1999) 70 locations at peak.

Red Barn (1961-1986). 400 at peak

Roadhouse Grill (1992-2008) 20 locations at peak

Royal Castle (1938–1975) 100 locations at peak

S & W Cafeteria (1920 - 2011) 16 locations at peak

Sambo's Restaurants -1957. Had over 1,100 locations by 1980. Renamed "No Place Like Sam's" then "Jolly Tiger." Sambo's said it took its name from its founders names – **Sam** Battistone and Newell F. **Boh**nett, but the name also meant a derogatory term to African-Americans.

Schrafft's (1906-1979) About 50 locations at its peak

Sisters Chicken & Biscuits (initially owned by Wendy's) (1978–1994)

Steak and Ale Restaurants (1966–2008). Peaked in 1992 with 157 restaurants.

Sweet Tomatoes/Souplantation (1978–2020) 97 locations at peak

Two Pesos (1982–1993) Unknown number at peak

Valle's Steak House, (1933-2000). 32 locations at its peak.

Velvet Turtle – (Unknown start–1993). 22 locations at its peak

Victoria Station (1969-1987) 100 locations at its peak

VIP's, (1969-1989). Had more than 50 at peak. In 1982 Denny's bought many.

Wag's – owned by Walgreen's. 91 at its peak. Sold to Marriott in 1988.

Wetson's, (1959–1975). Had over 70 locations.

White Tower (1926 – 2004) 230 locations at its peak

Wimpy's, (Opened in the US in 1934-1978). Still open in Europe and South Africa.

York Steak House (1966–1989) 200 at its peak. One still open in Columbus, Ohio.

Biggest Family-Owned Restaurant Chains

Chick-fil-A 1946 by Truett Cathy. (Dan T. Cathy, Chairman, Andrew Cathy, CEO, Donald Cathy, Executive Vice President, and Trudy Cathy White, Ambassador)

In-N-Out Burger. Started in 1948, In-N-Out was the first restaurant in California to have drive-thru service. Over 350 locations. (Lynsi Lavelle Snyder-Ellingson)

Lettuce Entertain You (LEYE) Based in Chicago that owns, manages and licenses more than 130 establishments in Illinois, Minnesota, Maryland, Nevada, California, Texas, Virginia, Florida, and Washington D.C. Founded in June 1971 by Richard Melman and Jerry A. Orzoff. It presently has more than 60 concepts and 125 restaurants ranging from fast casual to fine dining restaurants. (Richard Melman).

Pal's Sudden Service, founded in 1956 by Fred "Pal" Barger. 30 locations. Owned by the Barger family.

Panda Express over 2,200 locations (Peggy and Andrew Cherng)

Shari's Café and Pies Mostly on the West Coast, started in 1978. Has 95 locations across the Western United States. (Ron and Sharon Bergquist)

Largest Size Fast-Food Restaurant Locations

Arby's, Colonial Heights, Virginia

Bojangles, Charlotte, North Carolina
Has 5,000-square-feet.

Burger King, Budapest, Hungary
Has 3 levels with 15,000 square feet. For comparison, the average Burger King is 2,800 square feet.

Chick-fil-A, Midtown, New York
Has three levels and 12,000 sq ft, with 84 seats, 10 registers, two kitchens, no drive-thru window, but it does have a roof-top terrace.

Chipotle, Puteaux, France
7,000 square feet location seats 150 people and has dining on two floors.

Dairy Queen, Riyadh, Saudi Arabia

KFC, Baku, Azerbaijan
The largest KFC in the world opened in 2012. It is housed in an historic train station built in 1926. It has over 17,000 square foot, seats 300 people, and plans to sell 1.5 million meals a year.

McDonald's, Orlando, Florida
The largest McDonalds is located in Orlando, Florida. Opened in 1976 and renovated in 2016. Three-story, 19,000-square-foot building has children's play area, more than 50 arcade games, and is open 24 hours every day.

The Restaurant Compendium for the Curious

Sonic, Cheektowaga, New York
   Inside seating for 100 with 20 drive-in bays.

Starbucks Roastery, Manhattan, New York
   Opened in 2018. 20,000-square-foot Roastery in Manhattan located in a nine-story building.

Subway, Jamestown, North Carolina
   6,668 square feet location seats 211 people.

Wendy's, Tbilisi, Georgia
   15,000 square feet on three floors. It has a party hall, game zone, and a Wendy's Cafe serving 15 different kinds of coffee.

Multi-unit Chain Lifecycle Stages

Stage 1 Entrepreneurial

- Recognizes a market need
- Opens one location; Most owners stay at this stage
- Low barriers to entry (but also easy for competitors)
- No patents or services protection, pretty much only protection is service marks to protect name
- Entrepreneur pays high personal price with working many hours and usually low compensation
- Most important is to generate word of mouth advertising (most effective and least expensive)
- Entrepreneur intimately involved with all details

Stage 2 Multi Unit Rationalization

Once potential is proven, can add restaurants

- Multi-unit skills are developed
- Decision to franchise or not
- Capital costs, operating costs and sales are better known, so financing with banks becomes doable as the concept proves itself
- Founding entrepreneur usually delegates the operations to trusted manager
- New units drain talent away from existing units
- Employee morale is high, ground floor of opportunity
- Most sites still selected by founder
- Decision to advertise is usually because of ego of owner rather

than good reasons.
- Good performance increases probability that customers' loyalty is to the brand, not just to a restaurant.

Stage 3 Growth

Once a restaurant proves that its concept is profitable and reproducible, rapid expansion follows. Can grow by purchase of competitors, franchising, construction of new company owned restaurants, or combination of all the above

- Growth needs large amount of cash to finance construction and initial operating deficits
- Large lenders become interested in funding growth or can go public with IPO
- Systems must have capability to add new units with minimum of trouble
- Develops more formal structure, usually geographically
- Morale is high, because of fast promotions
- Some of the restaurants suffer first decline of sales; Need to remodel older units
- Advertising agency used
- Tasks must be separated (Finance, operations, marketing)
- Entrepreneur forced to manage by numbers

Stage 4 Mature

- Growth rate slows and unit sales decline
- Loses uniqueness
- Intensive marketing campaigns to differentiate

- Franchise restaurants lose consistency as franchisees become more dissatisfied
- Morale goes down since growth is slow and promotions are fewer and slower
- Managers leave since few opportunities
- Difficult to attract good managers in slow/non-growth stage
- Maintaining standards of the company is priority
- Need to remodel older units
- Few founders last beyond growth stage
- Doubts about the viability of concept

Stage 5 Decline or Regeneration

Regeneration:
- Find untapped markets for its present concept
- Execute successful changes to present concept
- Develop new concept
- Acquire new concept

Decline:
- Until the above happens, the company will stay in a stage of decline and deterioration
- Once tailspin begins, very difficult to pull out
- Management has serious doubts about making further investment in the company

The Restaurant Compendium for the Curious

BEST RESTAURANT MISSION STATEMENTS

Note – Mission statements are different from vision statements. Vision statements are usually vague and idealistic, while the mission statements are more specific.

What makes a "best" mission statement?

Short, to the point, makes employees proud, can be easily remembered and quoted. But the real test is if the mission statement influences corporate decisions.

Ben and Jerry's: Making the best possible ice cream, in the nicest possible way

Starbucks – To inspire and nurture the human spirit – one person, one cup and one neighborhood at a time

Sweetgreen: To inspire healthier communities by connecting people to real food

Worst Mission Statements
What qualifies as "worst"?

When no one can tell what business the company is in, generic, wordy, and obviously treated as just a task to get done.

Denny's: To establish beneficial business relationships with diverse suppliers who share our commitment to exceptional quality, excellent customer service, and competitive pricing.

Wendy's: Deliver superior quality products and services for our customers and communities through leadership, innovation, and partnerships.

A Few Chain Mission Statements

Arby's: To provide an exceptional dining experience that satisfies our guests' grown-up tastes by being a "Cut-Above" in everything we do

BJ's Restaurants: Our genuine commitment is to take pride in passionately connecting with every guest, on every visit, through flawless and relentless execution of every detail during every shift – to create and keep fanatical fans of BJ's concept and brand.

Buffalo Wild Wings: To WOW people every day!

Chick-Fil-A: To be America's best quick-service restaurant at winning and keeping customers

Chili's: To deliver Fresh Tex and Fresh Mex flavors like no place else. Our passion is making people feel special. We want you to leave Chili's feeling better than when you came in.

Chipotle: Food with integrity

Del Frisco's Restaurant Group: Do right and far exceed expectations daily. We do the right thing and lead by putting people first. Each and every connection with our team, guests and shareholders is our opportunity to create an experience that FEEDs – Far Exceeds Expectations Daily – and show how much we care.

Disney: To entertain, inform, and inspire people around the globe through the power of unparalleled storytelling; reflecting the iconic brands, creative minds, and innovative technologies that make ours the world's premier entertainment company.

Domino's Pizza: Is a company of exceptional people on a mission to be the best pizza delivery company in the world

Dunkin' – Everything we do is about you. From chefs who create exciting new flavors, to crew members who know exactly how you want your drink—we prioritize what you need to get you on your way. We strive to keep you at your best, and we remain loyal to you, your tastes and your time. That's what America runs on.

Habit Burger: To become everyone's favorite Habit, one burger at a time.

Houston's (Hillstone): We strive to create a comfortable atmosphere where you can focus on relaxing with friends and loved ones, knowing you'll always be taken care of.

In-N-Out Burgers: Serve only the highest quality product, prepare it in a clean and sparkling environment, and serve it in a warm and friendly manner.

Jack in the Box: To make the world a more delicious place.

Krispy Kreme: To make the most awesome doughnuts on the planet every single day.

McDonald's: To make delicious feel-good moments easy for everyone.

Olive Garden: We want the experience of warmth and caring to extend beyond our restaurant walls and into every community where we live and serve.

Pal's Sudden Service: Delight customers in a way that creates loyalty.

Panda Express: To deliver exceptional Asian dining experiences by building an organization where people are inspired to better their lives.

P.F. Chang's: Celebrate Life. Family. Food.

Papa John's: Will create superior brand loyalty, i.e. "raving fans," through (a) authentic, superior-quality products, (b) legendary customer service and (c) exceptional community service.

Red Lobster: We've been committed to bringing you a seafood experience you won't find anywhere else. That's how we Sea Food Differently

Red Robin: We take great care in choosing the people who take great care of you. From our servers to our chefs to our greeters, we're all about making sure you have a good time, every time.

Ruby Tuesday's: Quality. Passion. Pride.

Shake Shack – We Stand for Something Good in everything we do: This means carefully sourced premium ingredients from like-minded purveyors we admire and love; thoughtful, well-crafted and responsible design for its place; and deep community support through donations, events and volunteering.

TGI Fridays: In here, it's always Friday.

Waffle House: To deliver a unique experience to our customers through delivering great food, friendly, attentive service, excellent price, and a welcoming presence.

Wayback Burgers: To create a culture of belonging by uniting people through the love of comfort food.

Wingstop: To serve the world flavor.

Doesn't fit here, but still love it
Panera Bread's Cultural values
1. No jerks
2. Rule #1
3. No shortcuts
4. Profit

ON MANAGING

Chain Restaurant Managing Environment

General Managers of chain restaurants have more flexibility in how they run their restaurants than you might think. They are basically encouraged to manage as if they were the owner. However, unlike an owner, they can't change some aspects, but they can change some, and they can change some a lot.

Cannot change:
- Hours of operation
- Menu unless allowed to do a "special"
- Recipes
- Ways you handle money/charge cards, checks, gift certificates, etc.
- Accounting and money
- Must follow chain of command
- Pay and benefits
- Each manager will have a budget $ or % for each category of area of responsibility

"The Rules"
- One manager or supervisor must be present at all times in the restaurant
- Cannot unilaterally fire an assistant manager (must get district supervisor involved)
- Always communicate serious incidents with immediate boss

(no surprises)

- Cannot spend more than a set amount (often $500 - $1,000) without approval from immediate boss, unless it is normal operating expenses, such as for food, liquor, beer, wine or supplies

- Each manager works towards a budget for their individual department. Every dollar spent goes into the P & L (profit and loss statement), so that each manager is accountable for his/her area.

- Must receive an "A" on health inspections

- Responsible for morale, cleanliness, and costs

General Manager Flexibility (manager's discretion)
- Authority of assistant managers

- Discipline standards (from lax to strict and in between)

- Organization of restaurant

- Staffing

- Scheduling of assistants, staff and yourself (unless have specific guidelines)

- Responsibilities of assistants

- Incentives, contests within budget

INSIDE THE INCREDIBLY COMPLEX FOOD AND BEVERAGE WORLDS OF HOSPITALS AND STADIUMS

Inside Hospital Foodservice

Imagine for a moment: you must feed hundreds of patients in hospital rooms 3 times per day with the exact dietary and portion requirements or it might, let's see, *kill* them.

At the same time, you must operate multiple full dining rooms for breakfast, lunch, and dinner plus auxiliary operations for coffee, snacks, and gifts across possibly multiple health centers. Sound easy? You're right. It's not.

Healthcare foodservice serves a wide range of customers of all ages and backgrounds, patients, staff, doctors, nurses, technicians, visitors, infants, children, adults, and elderly.

Healthcare Foodservice Factors:
Inspections and Regulations
Infection control and food regulations

Inside Restaurants

- Local health department inspections
- Centers for Medicare and Medicaid Services (CMS) inspections
- Accrediting agency, The Joint Commission inspections
- State licensing inspections
- Infection Control (IC) with monthly visits

Trends in healthcare foodservice
- Hotel style patient room service
- Cook-to-order
- Technology solutions
- Mobile phone ordering options and QR code menus
- Patient and foodservice customers convenience
- Ethnic food options
- Community outreach via teaching healthy cooking
- Plant based menus
- Taste with nutrition

Inside Football Stadium Foodservice
Mercedes-Benz Stadium, Atlanta, Georgia

- Seats – 71,000 – 75,000 depending on venue
- Club seats – 7,600
- Suites – 190
- Concession points of sale – 673
- Bars/restaurants - 24
- Beer taps – 1,264

Challenges of stadium foodservice management

Since sporting events are not held every day, it is impossible to have full time employees who are trained and available. The necessity to hire, train, and staff each event on a weekly basis is a serious challenge.

Now, multiply that by 673 different locations within the stadium. Now add time-outs, half times, and 7th inning stretches when business is busy. Super busy. Like it feels like the majority of the stadium wants a beer followed by nothing.

Then add to that the luxury service required of the suites with specialized, often customized food. Then nothing for a few days. Then start over. Hopefully, most of your staff comes back but, when they don't, hiring and training more staff to do it again. Each week.

Easy Peasy. Not.

More challenges

Alcohol sales means high potential for liability (serving to underage and inebriated fans)

Food service companies rent the facilities from the stadium owners who charge enormous rental fees, which the concession operators must get back by charging high prices.

Sports foodservice trends

Going cashless - Quicker and more secure than cash

Contactless, using phone app to order, quicker, no lines.

No more condiment area – difficult to keep filled, clean, and organized

Celebrity chefs

Local food and beer

Self-service drink refill stations

Robotic pizza making

VIP suites can have personalized orders throughout game, not just pre-order.

Draft beer replaced by canned beer – faster and less hassle and waste

Deliveries direct to stadium seat

IT'S ALL ABOUT THE MONEY

Big Mac Index

The Economist's index (also known as burgernomics) has tracked the price of McDonald's Big Mac since 1986 as a way to assess the purchasing power parity (PPP) of various currencies. The Big Mac is available in over 120 countries.

Restaurant Server Pay

Did you know that restaurant servers do not get paid the same? Well, they don't. For example, a server in Alabama gets paid $2.13 per hour, but a server in Washington State gets paid $13.69, while a server in Massachusetts gets paid $5.55.

States pay differently depending upon how each state treats tips.

Huh?

It all depends on something called, "Tip Credit" and upon the attitude that each state has towards business and employees.

Tip Credit

Tip credit is part of federal law that allows employers to pay tipped employees below the federal or state minimum wage. Customers make up the difference with tips.

The tip credit fundamentally changed tipping. Tips used to be a thank you from the customer to the server, but now, the tip subsidizes employers of tipped employees since part of employee wages is paid by customers via their tips, not the employers.

Typically, tip credit can only be used with employees who have direct contact with customers, (servers, hosts, bartenders, and bussers), but not employees who do not (cooks, prep people, and dishwashers) who are paid with no pay below minimum wage.

Tipped employees, even with tips included, have wages that typically fall in the bottom 25% of all U.S. wage earners. Research from 2015 (The High Public Cost of Low Wages by Jacobs, Perry, and MacGillvary) found that 52% of all fast-food employees receive some form of state or federal public assistance.

Average pay for restaurant employees in 2021

According to ZipRecruiter.com, the average annual pay for a Restaurant Worker in the United States was $21,470 a year. (ZipRecruiter)

According to Glassdoor.com, the average salary for a restaurant employee was $27,815 in United States. (Glassdoor)

According to Indeed.com, the average base salary was $12.77 per hour or $32,367 per year.

CEO to Employee Pay Ratios

Beginning in 2018, The Dodd–Frank Wall Street Reform and Consumer Protection Act requires publicly traded companies to report a "pay ratio" which is the ratio between the CEO and the median employee. Note: Median is defined as halfway between the highest and lowest.

Example: Employee gets $2,000 per month; CEO gets $10,000 per month. Because the CEO gets 5 times more than the employee, the ratio would be 5:1

In the 1950's, the average CEO was paid about 20 times more than the typical worker's pay, going to 42-to-1 in 1980, then to 120-to-1 in 2000, and really increased in the last 10 years.

The city of Portland, Oregon passed a surtax in 2016 on companies whose CEOs earn more than 100 times the median pay of their employees.

Did You Know?

Ben & Jerry's Ice Cream originally capped the pay ratio of its CEO at 5:1, later raising the ratio to 7:1. Ben & Jerry's abandoned that rule in 1994 when the company couldn't find anyone to replace Ben Cohen upon his retirement.

As a Point of Reference
The ratio in the US military is about 6 to 1.
(O-8, major general to E-2, private 1st class)

Highest paid restaurant CEOs in 2020 (publicly traded)
(Includes salary, stock, bonuses, other)
according to proxy statements filed for the 2020 fiscal year

Full-Service Restaurants

YUM Brands (KFC, Taco Bell, The Habit Burger Grill) $10,113,748 (ratio 1,286:1)

Darden restaurants (Olive Garden, LongHorn Steakhouse, Cheddar's Scratch Kitchen, Bahama Breeze, Seasons 52, The Capital Grille, Eddie V's, and Yard House) $8,688,707 (Ratio 567:1)

Brinker International $6,958,837 (Ratio 364:1)

Cracker Barrel $6,216,441 (ratio 223:1)

Cheesecake Factory $5,914,037 (ratio 212:1)

Brinker International (Chilis, Maggiano's, It's Just Wings, and Maggiano's Italian Classics) $5,883,000 (ratio 211:1)

Bloomin' Brands (Bonefish Grill, Carrabba's Italian Grill, Fleming's Prime Steakhouse & Wine Bar, Outback Steakhouse, and Roy's) $5,576,984 (ratio 200:1)

Denny's $5,340,240 (ratio 192:1)

Red Robin $4,319,504 (ratio 155:1)

Texas Roadhouse $3,620,939 (ratio 130:1)

Quick-Service Restaurants

Chipotle $38,035,868 (ratio 1,368:1)

RBI Restaurant Brands International (Burger King, Tim Horton's, Popeye's, Firehouse Subs) $20,054,416 (ratio 721:1)

Starbucks $14,665,575 (ratio 527:1)

Yum! Brands (Pizza Hut, Taco Bell, KFC, Habit Burger) $14,631,451 (ratio 526:1)

McDonald's $10,847,032 (ratio 390:1)

Wendy's $7,213,774 (ratio 259:1)

Papa John's $6,378,193 (ratio 229:1)

Domino's $6,295,230 (ratio 226:1)

Wingstop $6,010,462 (ratio 216:1)

Jack in the Box $5,855,701 (ratio 210:1)

State Minimum Hourly Wages for Tipped Employees

Federal minimum wage is $7.25 per hour. Federal minimum wage for tipped employees is $2.13 per hour with tip credit

States With Highest Pay for Tipped Employees

States requiring employers to pay tipped employees the *full* state minimum wage *plus* tips

Alaska $10.34

California based on number of employees: 25 or fewer employees $13;

26 or more employees $14

Minnesota based on sales: sales of less than $500,000 $8.21 More than $500,000 $10.08

Montana based on sales: less than $110,000 $4.00, more than $110,000 $8.75

Nevada $9.75

Oregon $12.75

Washington $13.69

States With Lowest Pay for Tipped Employees
State minimum cash wage payment is the same as federal law

Alabama $2.13
Georgia $2.13
Indiana $2.13
Kansas $2.13
Kentucky 2.13
Louisiana 2.13
Mississippi $2.13
Nebraska $2.13
North Carolina $2.13
South Carolina $2.13
Tennessee $2.13
Texas $2.13
Utah $2.13
Virginia $2.13
Wyoming $2.13

States Between Highest and Lowest Pay for Tipped Employees

States requiring employers to pay tipped employees *above* the federal minimum wage, *but not* the full state minimum wage

The Restaurant Compendium for the Curious

Arizona $9.15
Arkansas $2.63
Colorado $9.30
Connecticut
Delaware $2.23
Idaho $3.35
Illinois $6.60
Iowa $4.35
Maine $6.08
Maryland $3.63
Massachusetts $5.55
Michigan $3.67
Missouri $5.15
New Hampshire $3.26
New Jersey $4.13
North Dakota $4.86
Ohio $4.40
Pennsylvania $2.83
Rhode Island $3.89
South Dakota $4.72
Vermont $5.87
West Virginia $2.62
Wisconsin $2.33

Forbes World's Best Restaurant Chains to Work For

October 11, 2022
177 AmRest (Spain)
268 Starbucks (US)
357 Papa John's (US)
570 Subway (US)
604 Five Guys (US)
649 Group Le Duff (France)

Glassdoor Best Places to Work For 2022

One restaurant chain in top 100
39 **In-N-Out** – benefits and opportunities for advancement

TIPPING

Pros and Cons of Tipping in Restaurants

Pros:
Keeps costs down for owners and menu prices down for customers

Tips can provide large earning potential, especially in high volume or high-priced restaurants. Many servers thrive knowing that their service can have a direct impact on their earnings

Cons:
Research has found that using tips as a measure of performance is ineffective with little to no correlation between tips and performance (M. Lynn, 2001).

Pros and Cons of No Tipping in Restaurants

Raising the minimum wage and eliminating tips are two of the most polarizing issues in the restaurant industry. No-tipping restaurants would have to increase menu prices, but guests realistically wouldn't pay more overall since they would no longer tip.

Pros:
There is often friction between the front and back of house staff because servers can often make double what the kitchen staff makes. But most would agree that the kitchen is just as important to the customer experience as service, especially with take-out. Having pay that is more equal might reduce friction and might raise service and reduce turnover,

Cons:

The tipping culture in American restaurants is strong. Customers are used to rewarding good service and servers love the extra money. Eliminating tipping might alienate customers which could backfire and cause customers to go elsewhere.

Current tipped employees would resent losing tips and might also make servers reluctant to work busy shifts since they're making the same money on slower, less stressful shifts.

BAD STUFF

Pandemics, Depressions, Recessions, Flus, Diseases, and Lawsuits. Besides that, we're good.

Food Poisoning and Restaurants

1993 Jack in the Box (E. Coli from undercooked hamburgers) 4 died, 700 + sick, mostly in Seattle area. Paid out more than $50 million

2003 Chi-Chi's (Hepatitis-A from raw green onions) 3 deaths, 555 sick. Paid out $800,000 in a class action settlement to 9,000 people plus millions to individual victims who suffered serious health issues. Total of $40 million.

2006 Taco Bell (E. Coli in shredded lettuce) 0 deaths, 71 sick.

2015-2018 Chipotle Mexican Grill (Norovirus, salmonella, E. coli) 0 deaths, 1,100 sick. Improved food safety program paid $25 million criminal fee.

Food Borne Diseases

- Salmonella (most common cause of food poisoning in US)

- E. Coli
- Hepatitis A
- Listeria
- Norovirus
- Clostridium perfringens
- Campylobacter
- Staphylococcus aureus (Staph)
- Botulism

The Pandemic's Effects on the Restaurant Industry
The pandemic is the cause of several trends

2019 and 2020 were brutal on the restaurant industry, particularly full-service restaurants. According to the National Restaurant Association, 17% of restaurants in the US closed. The restaurant industry lost more than $130 billion in sales and over 2 million jobs. Quick-service restaurants, especially those with drive-up service, were able to adapt more easily to the restrictions of the pandemic than full-service restaurants that had to rely on in-person customers.

Because of restrictions, many restaurants were forced to close because sales were so low. The pandemic brought rising food costs, supply chain problems, severe staffing shortages, difficulty in paying staff, and paying bills. As a result, restaurants reduced hours of operation and closed days when they would have been open. Some restaurants started food delivery, contactless transactions, reduced their menus, accepted online ordering, emphasis on drive-thrus, outdoor dining, and increased social media to keep in customer contact. COVID-19 accelerated restaurant using technology and social media. Even though employee wages and benefits have gone up, the restaurant industry's number one issue remains recruiting and retaining employees.

Federal government assistance helped prevent even worse carnage

During COVID-19, the U.S. government provided lifelines to restaurants harmed by closures, but for many restaurants, it was not enough. Paycheck Protection Program (PPP), run by the Small Business Administration, gave out roughly $800 billion dollars in low-interest loans.

The Restaurant Revitalization Fund gave out $28.6 billion, approved 101,000 applications, and turned down 177,000 applications.

Possible trends:
- Good drive-through properties are in high demand, even bank properties with drive-thrus are being looked at as possible restaurant conversions.
- Drive- through restaurants in fast food have done well, causing casual, full-service restaurants to consider adding.
- Curb side pick-up will continue to be strong.
- Since working from home will continue, restaurant sales could suffer since people won't get breakfast or coffee on the way to work, get lunch with their work buddies, or get together after work for happy hour.

Trying Times for Restaurants

1918 Flu pandemic and WW I

More U.S. soldiers died from the flu than were killed during WW I and about 675,000 people died from the virus in the United States alone. During the pandemic, many restaurants, saloons, and other public eating places throughout the country were forced to close because of local health restrictions.

World War I caused more than 4 million potential restaurant customers to be sent overseas as soldiers and sailors before a ceasefire and Armistice was declared on November 11, 1918. With so many customers gone, restaurant sales declined. This was bad, but this was just the beginning. The Spanish Flu pandemic hit bringing another serious blow to restaurants.

Differences Between the 1918 Flu and the 2019 COVID-19

The National Restaurant Association reported that there are approximately a million restaurants in the United States, but in 1918, there were at most 100,000 restaurants.

In 1915, about 50% of all Americans lived in rural areas; today, it's less than 20%. Restaurants need a certain density of population with disposable income. In 1918, restaurants mainly catered to the huge numbers of people who had moved from rural farmland to cities and lived in one-room studios or boarding houses with no kitchens. In 1918, homeownership was the exception, not the rule and take-out did not exist. And believe it or not, no delivery or drive-ins. The horrors.

There were other major differences. During the 1918 Flu Pandemic, most health measures were local rather than federal and, unlike today, there was no federal restaurant assistance during the Spanish Flu.

While virtual brands were becoming more popular before the pandemic, the boom of takeout and delivery orders during the health crisis led more restaurants to add virtual restaurants. For many companies, virtual brands and take-out were the only positives during closures. In the 12 months ended March 2021, U.S. restaurant digital orders grew 124%, according to the NPD Group.

The 1930's Great Depression

"Penny restaurants" grew popular, with everything on the menu costing less than a dollar, with many items on the menu literally costing one penny. These restaurants helped preserve the dignity of people since they did pay, not just accepted charity. The depression also caused lunch counters to open in big department stores.

Prohibition (1920-1933)

One of the unintended consequences of prohibition was the closure of many restaurants because of their dependence on alcohol sales.

Biggest Personal Injury Lawsuits

1975 Chi Chi's
The largest hepatitis A outbreak in the United States with 660 people falling ill and four deaths happened in Chi-Chis. The cause was raw green onions in the salsa. Chi-Chi's had to pay $800,000 in a class action lawsuit and millions to individual lawsuits with a total of $40 million paid out.

1991 Cracker Barrel
The CEO and founder, Dan Evins, issued a company-wide directive to fire any employee "whose sexual preferences fail to demonstrate normal heterosexual values." Because of that directive, 16 employees were fired. His reasoning was that gay people made customers in rural areas feel uncomfortable. The New York City Employees Retirement System, which owned more than $6 million of Cracker Barrel shares, encouraged other stockholders to use their votes to organize resistance. Evins later apologized and retracted the directive.

1993 Jack in the Box
Had an E. coli outbreak causing 732 people to fall ill and 4 children to die. The cause was undercooked hamburger patties. Jack in the Box and Foodmaker, parent company of Jack in the Box, had to pay out $15.6 million.

1994 Denny's
Paid out more than $54 million to settle lawsuits filed by thousands of African American customers. This was the largest settlement ever made under US public accommodation laws. As a result, Denny's hired more African American managers. Denny's has stated that it will help the Multicultural Foodservice & Hospitality Alliance (MFHA) ato achieve its goal of 100 black-owned franchises by 2023.

1994 McDonald's
Jury awarded Stella Liebeck (81) $2.9 million who, in 1992, ordered a 49-cent cup of coffee at a drive-in window and received third-degree burns when she removed the lid to add cream and sugar and spilled the scalding hot coffee onto her lap. She spent 7 days in the hospital getting skin grafts and two years of medical visits. During the trial, it came out that 700 others had complained about injuries from hot coffee. The judge in the case reduced the jury award to $500,000.

1994 Checkers
A French fry cracked a tooth and was awarded $550,000.

1997 Burger King
An E. coli outbreak sickened 16 people in Colorado. 1,650 restaurants in 28 states had to take burgers off their menus. Burger Kings beef processor had to recall more than 25 million pounds of beef.

1997 Hooters Gender Discrimination
Hooter's paid $3.75 million to settle a sexual discrimination lawsuit brought by men turned down for jobs because of their gender. The settlement allows Hooters to continue to have female Hooters Girls exclusively, but the chain agreed to create a few other support jobs, such as bartenders and hosts, that must be filled without regard to gender.

2002 McDonald's
Inaccurately labeled French fries and hash browns as vegetarian. McDonald's issued an apology and paid $10 million to vegetarian and religious groups for using beef flavoring in its French fries and hash browns.

2006 Taco Bell
More than 70 people in 4 states got E. Coli with 53 requiring hospitalizations. The cause was found to be shredded lettuce. Lawsuits totaled more than $76 million.

2009 Starbucks
Howard Shultz and the board of directors approved a $100 million settlement in back tips in a barista-led class action lawsuit in

California.

2022 Cracker Barrel
Was ordered by a jury to pay $9.4 million over a lawsuit involving a Tennessee customer who drank what he believed to be a glass of water in 2014, but which turned out to be a cleaning fluid. The jury awarded $4.3 million in compensatory damages and $5 million in punitive damages. The award may be reduced, however, due to a $750,000 limit on damages in Tennessee law.

Most Common Restaurant Lawsuits

1. **Slip and Falls.** Liability suits claiming personal injury due to the property owner's negligence are common in restaurants. Common causes:
   - Wet floor: Restaurants often have food and drink spills and cooking oil drips. Mopping also creates wet surfaces that can cause falls.
   - Low light: Restaurants typically have reduced lighting to create a pleasant and relaxing ambiance. This dimly lit atmosphere may make it difficult for customers to see obstacles or hazards.
   - Uneven floor: If a section of a floor is not level or has an unexpected step, people may fall.

2. **Altercation Claims.** Because restaurants serve alcohol, customers can sometimes start fights between guests or between a staff member and a guest.

3. **Alcohol-Related Cases.** Dram Shop laws govern injury claims from people who purchase alcohol at a restaurant or bar, become intoxicated, and cause an accident resulting in injuries. Third-party claims happen when an intoxicated person causes damage to another individual. First-party cases happen when the plaintiff is the person who purchased and got intoxicated. Many states do not allow first-party claims unless the claimant is a minor.

4. Employment Practices Suits
- Employees not paid on time
- Lack of breaks during their shifts
- Employees do not receive at least minimum wage
- Unpaid overtime: Employees must work off the clock

5. Food Poisoning

CRISES OF RESTAURANT CHAINS

Chick-Fil-A Beliefs (2012)

What happened?

In 2012, the CEO of Chick-Fil-A publicly expressed his religious views and opposition to same sex marriage. He said, "We operate on biblical principles," and donated millions to anti-gay groups who opposed gay marriage.

The statement caused backlash from the gay community and friends of the gay community.

- Many mayors wanted to ban Chick-fil-A's from coming into their cities
- Many universities petitioned to have them kicked off campus
- Celebrities promised to boycott

- Lots of negative publicity

Chick-Fil-A's response:
- "The Chick-Fil-A culture and service tradition in our restaurants is to treat every person with honor, dignity and respect—regardless of belief, creed and sexual orientation. Going forward, our intent is to leave the policy debate over same-sex marriage to the government and political arena. "

- For many months now, Chick-fil-A's corporate giving has been mischaracterized, and while our sincere intent has been to remain out of this political and social debate, events from Chicago have once again resulted in questions around our giving. For that reason, we want to provide some context and clarity around who we are, what we believe and our priorities in relation to corporate giving. A part of our corporate commitment is to be responsible stewards of all that God has entrusted to us. Because of this commitment, Chick-fil-A's giving heritage is focused on programs that educate youth, strengthen families, enrich marriages, and support communities. We will continue to focus our giving in those areas. Our intent is not to support political or social agendas.

The issues
- Risk in CEO stating publicly beliefs on social issues

- Risk in loss of customers (gays, friends of gays, etc.)

- Corporations have the right to take political stances on social issues, but customers have the right not to visit.

- Private companies CEOs, like Chick-Fil-A, do not have to answer to shareholders, while the CEO of a public company does.

Applebee's Tip Policy (2013)

What happened?
A party of nine came in and was given the bill which included an

automatic gratuity of 18%
- The customer, a pastor, crossed out the automatic gratuity and wrote on the receipt" I give God 10%, why do you get 18%?"
- The server took a picture of the receipt and uploaded it to Reddit.
- The pastor found out about the posting and called the GM, who fired the server.
- The server's post went viral

Applebee's side
- Applebee's responded on Facebook that the server had violated the guest's right to privacy
- By that afternoon, 10,000 negative comments appeared online, by 2am, 17,000 comments had appeared on Facebook

What did Applebee's do?
- Started to delete negative comments
- Blocked people from their Facebook page and started arguing with them
- This caused many more negative comments
- 5am: "Please let us assure you that Applebee's and every one of our franchisees values our hard-working team member and the amazing job they do serving our guests. We recognize the extraordinary effort required and the tremendous contribution they make and appreciate your recognition and support of our colleagues."

By noon the next day:
- Applebee's status update with 20,000 comments is deleted
- Applebee's then posts: "No posts have been deleted"
- It got 1.4 million views

Subway Footlong (2013)

What happened

A customer in Australia put a picture of a Subway footlong with a tape measure that clearly showed that it was only 11 inches and not 12 inches long. He posted on Subway's Facebook page with "Subway, please respond"

Customer reaction

Picture went viral. It had 100,000 likes almost immediately. Customers started bringing tape measures to Subway, complaining, posting pictures, etc.

Next day, Chain's 1st response:

"Subway's 'SUBWAY FOOTLONG' is a registered trademark and not intended to be a measurement of length."

This was obviously written by lawyers which didn't even pass the "smile" test. This hurt their credibility and added to the crisis. Most people were amused at first, but this made people mad. Either it is called a footlong as a name and it is *not* supposed to be a foot long OR it *should* be a foot long but didn't meet standards. Both statements can't be true. By not putting out the small crisis immediately, Subway turned a one-inch nuisance into a disaster.

Chain's 2nd response:

"We are committed to providing the same amount of bread with every order. The length however may vary slightly when not baked to our exact specifications. We are reinforcing our policies and procedures in an effort to ensure our offerings are always consistent."

As part of the settlement, Subway agreed to ensure that for at least four years its bread will be at least 12 inches long. The judge approved $520,000 in lawyers' fees and $500 for each of the 10 individuals who brought the class action, but no monetary claims were awarded. Subway could have had fun with this and gotten massive positive PR out of it, but they chose another path.

Domino's Pizza Gross Out (2009)

What happened?

A small Domino's franchise in North Carolina had 2 employees post a prank video to YouTube of them doing very disgusting things to Domino's pizzas and sending the pizzas out to customers.

Customer reaction:

The video went viral, from 20,000 views to 760,000 views within hours. Two days later, there were one million views. Within 48 hours, Domino's brand quality went from positive to negative.

Two days later, Domino's responded by removing the video from YouTube and fired the two employees. It issued this statement: "The opportunities and freedom of the internet is wonderful," the statement reads. "But it also comes with the risk of anyone with a camera and an internet link to cause a lot of damage, as in this case, where a couple of individuals suddenly overshadow the hard work performed by the 125,000 men and women working for Domino's across the nation and in 60 countries around the world."

There were at least three problems. Domino's waited 48 hours to respond which is way too long, especially after over a million people had seen the video. In this age of instant communications, it was 23 hours too long.

Second, it took way too long to get the video removed from YouTube and third, evidently there was no manager or supervisor around during the filming.

Hooters Weight Discrimination Lawsuit (2010)

A former Hooters employee in a Detroit suburb sued Hooters, alleging she was unable to keep her job after being told to lose weight. In a performance evaluation, management put her on 30-day "weight probation" and advised her to join a gym to improve her looks and fit into her required uniform. The official uniform for Hooters waitresses, she claims, comes in 3 sizes: extra extra small, extra small, or small.

Hooters then told the other employees what had happened, creating an "intensely humiliating, deeply offensive, untenable" work environment, forcing her to resign, according to the lawsuit.

Before this performance evaluation, she had received good reviews and a promotion to shift leader, the complaint said. According to the complaint, she is 5'8" tall and weighs 132.5 pounds, down from 145 pounds when she was recruited for employment in 2008.

Hooters' conduct violated a Michigan law barring discrimination on the basis of weight, the complaint said. Hooters settled this lawsuit in arbitration.

The Borgata Casino Weight Discrimination (2013)

According to a controversial ruling by a Superior Court judge in New Jersey, casino waitresses are essentially "sex objects" (a direct quote), who can be terminated for gaining weight.

The decision by Superior Court Judge Nelson Johnson ended a workplace discrimination and wrongful termination lawsuit brought by 20 former cocktail waitresses against the Atlantic City casino, The Borgata.

The women, known disparagingly as the "Borgata Babes," brought their suit against the Borgata Hotel Casino & Spa for weight discrimination. The women were specifically contesting a workplace policy at the casino banning "Borgata Babes" from gaining anything over 7% of the body weight recorded on their date of their hire.

In Johnson's ruling, the judge argued that Borgata's guidelines were both legal and fair, and that women should know what kind of position they're accepting when they apply for a position with the casino.

Celebrity Chef's Employees (2014)

1,050 employees filed a class action suit against Michelin starred chef, Daniel Boulud. The suit claimed that the chef had not properly compensated them for the work they did, that he pocketed their tips, and that he forced tipped employees to pool tips with kitchen staff. The restaurant had to pay $1.4 million. But. After they paid their lawyers, each employee received about $889.

Countries That Still Have Restaurants That Serve Cats and Dogs
According to the Humane Society and Four Paws

China- 10-20 million dogs and cats

Vietnam – 5 million dogs and cats

South Korea – 2 million. According to DW.com, fewer than 100 restaurants serve dogs in Seoul in 2019

Indonesia – 1 million dogs and cats

Philippines – 500,000 dogs

Thailand – Illegal to consume dogs, but legal to traffic to Vietnam

Laos – trafficked to Vietnam

Cambodia- trafficked to Vietnam

In 1998, Taiwan was the first Asian country to ban eating dogs and cats. Their Animal Protection Act states that anyone selling, eating, or buying the animals for consumption face fines of up to $8,200.

Those found guilty of animal cruelty could also receive a fine of $65,000 and two years in prison.

THE BUSINESS OF RESTAURANTS

Trade Dress or I'm So Pretty

Trade dress is the legal and formal name of the distinctive appearance and décor of a restaurant. Besides the name, trade dress is one of the *few* areas of a restaurant that can be protected. To gain common law protection under the Lanham Act, trade dress must be "distinctive." This means that consumers perceive a particular trade dress as uniquely identifying. For example, think of the red and white stripes of TGI Fridays. Two that went to court were Two Pesos vs Taco Cabana and The Amazon Bar & Grill vs Rainforest Café.

Myth – 90% of restaurants fail in the first year
Real Failure Rate of Restaurants

Peer reviewed research (Parsa, Self, Njite, and King, 2005) shows that the real failure rate for the first year is closer to 25%. Or to put it a better way, restaurants have around a 75% success rate the first year. After 3 years, the failure rate rises to around 60% and the restaurants that are still going after 3 years, tend to last.

Buying a Restaurant Franchise

Start-up investments usually include building improvements, equipment, fixtures, and furnishings, point-of-sales systems, signs, opening advertising, initial inventory, training assistance of management and employees, grand opening expenses, and some number of months of operating funds.

Many restaurant franchisors require multi-year, multi-restaurant deals within a specific geographic area and within a specific period of time.

- **Applebee's** – $40,000 franchise fee, 4% royalty fee, 4.2% advertising fee. Requires an initial investment between $2 million-$9.9 million. Franchisees are generally required to have about $1 million in net worth for each restaurant they plan to open.

- **Auntie Anne's:** Franchise fee $35,000, 7% royalty fee, 1%-3% advertising fee. Initial investment between $146,000-$524,000. Between $300,000-$580,000 net worth, with $120,000-$260,000 liquid cash.

- **Baskin Robbins:** Franchise fee of $25,000, 5.9% royalty fee, 5% advertising fee. Must have net worth of $200,000 with $100,000 liquid cash. Total initial investment between $294,000-$626,000

- **Burger King:** The franchise fee is $50,000, royalties are 4.5% of gross sales Costs from $300,000 to $3 million, depending on location. Franchisees are expected to have a net worth of $1.0 million and at least $500,000 cash liquidity.

- **Del Taco:** (1.6 million average annual sales) Franchise fee of $35,000, 5% royalty fee, 4% advertising fee. Total estimated initial investment between $812,000-$2.3million. Minimum net worth $2million with $500,000 liquid cash.

- **Denny's:** Franchise fee of $30,000, 4.5%-7% royalty fee. Minimum $500,000 liquid capital, $1 million net worth., $1.4-$2.3million total investment

- **DQ Grill & Chill:** Franchise fee of $45,000, 4% royalty fee, 5-6% marketing fee with $1.4-$2.4 million total investment range

- **Dunkin'** – Franchise fee of $40,000-$90,000, 2%-6% royalty fee, 5.0% advertising fee. Must have net worth of $500,000 and cash liquidity of $250,000

- **Jack in the Box** – Franchise fee of $50,000, 5% royalty fee, 5% marketing fee, with $1.6-$2.6 million total investment.

- **Krispy Kreme:** Franchise fee $25,000-$50,000, 4.5% royalty fee, up to 8.5% total advertising fees. Initial investment between $440,500-$1.2million. Must have net worth $2.0 million and liquid cash $300,000

- **McDonald's:** $45,000 franchise fee, 4% royalty fee, 4% advertising fee. Total investment between $1.36-$2.45 million.

- **Panda Express:** $25,000 franchise fee, 8.0% royalty fee, 0 advertising fee. Initial investment between $426,700-$2,404,000

- **Panera Bread-** Panera's royalties are 5% of gross sales. Initial startup costs from $816,886 to more than $2 million, excluding real estate costs. Equipment costs are estimated at about $185,000 to more than $310,000. The franchise fee is $35,000.

- **Papa Murphy's:** Franchise fee of $25,000, total investment between $308,000-$557,000 with minimum of $125,000 liquid cash.

- **Schlotzsky's:** Franchise fee of $35,500, 6.0% royalty fees, advertising 4% of net sales. Initial investment between $522,000-$1.6 million.

- **Taco Bell -** Franchise fee of $45,000, 5.5% royalty fee, 4.25% marketing fee, with $1.3-$3.3 million total investment. Must have net worth of $1.5million and cash liquidity of $750,000

- **Papa John's –** Franchise fee of $25,000, 5.0% royalty fee, 8% advertising fee, with a total investment of $130,000-$844,000. Must have net worth of $750,000 and cash liquidity of $250,000.

- **Whataburger –** Must agree to open at least 5 Whataburger restaurants within 5 years. Have at least $5 million in liquid assets and $12.5 million in net worth.

Significant Impacts and Massive Changes

Gone and Mainly Forgotten

All you can eat: Herb McDonald (no relation) usually gets credit for starting the first all-you-can-eat buffet (Buckaroo Buffet) in a Las Vegas casino in 1946. All-you-can-eat reached its peak popularity in the 1980s.

Cafeterias: These came into being when people started to work in factories and could not go home to have lunch. The cafeteria eliminated the server, making the service much faster. Get it and eat it. Maybe the first cafeteria in the US was the Exchange Buffet in New York City that opened in 1885. The Child's Cafeteria chain is usually credited with adding the tray line.

Dinner theaters: Pay one price for a full sit-down meal and a play. The first dinner theater in the US was probably the Barksdale Theater in 1953, but some credit Bill Pullinsi as the first when he started the Candlelight Dinner Playhouse in Chicago in 1959. Later, in 1961, Howard Wolfe, "the father of dinner theater" started the Barn Diner Theatre chain. The peak in popularity was in the 1970s when there were almost 150 professional dinner theaters in the United States.

Trends

AI (Artificial Intelligence): White Castle began using the first AI-powered robot to work in a fast-food kitchen. The robot is used to fry several menu items. The robot is named "Flippy."

Automation comes to the restaurant industry: just kidding.

Automobile assembly line efficiency comes to fast food: some say that the biggest change in the restaurant industry during the 20th century was when the McDonald brothers incorporated Henry

Ford's assembly line into making burgers. They could make their menu cheaper and faster than their competition because their simplified approach meant they could hire relatively inexpensive and unskilled employees.

Breakfast comes to fast food: Breakfast at a burger place? Impossible, never happen. Not so fast, grasshopper. In 1972, the Egg McMuffin, first sold in Belleville New Jersey, changed all that by adding a completely new meal period to fast food.

Credit cards come to fast food: Subway, McDonald's, and KFC began accepting credit cards in 2003 in at least some locations. Credit card transactions became as fast or faster than cash transactions, reduced mistakes, and the potential for embezzlement. Plus, people just want to use credit cards with the added benefit that most people spend more when using a credit card than when using cash.

Commute: The car becomes the dining room. Cereal used to be considered a fast meal, but not now. Cereal sales went down as commuting grew because it's tough to eat cereal in a car. As a result, milk sales fell too. Now, many fast-food chains only offer meals that require no utensils. Cars evolved with convenient and mandatory cup holders. Remember hanging cup holders on the a/c vents? Right. Me neither.

Drive-thru: In-N-Out (Harry and Esther Snyder) is usually credited with the first drive thru in 1948 when they installed two-way speaker boxes that made it so drivers didn't have to leave their cars. Jack-in-the-Box started drive-thru in 1951, Wienerschnitzel in 1961, and Wendy's had drive-thrus in 1969. Surprisingly, McDonald's and Burger King didn't start drive thru until 1975.

Franchising: According to IFA (International Franchise Association) the first modern franchise was probably when Martha Matilda Harper began franchising the Harper Method Shops in 1891, a hair care business that included training, branded products, field visits, advertising, group insurance and motivation. This grew to over 500 salons at its peak with the last one closing in 1972.

Restaurants joined franchising in 1919 when A&W Root Beer began franchising. (Brothers Sherman and J.W. Marriott were franchisees). Howard Johnson began franchising in 1935 after finding it impossible to obtain bank financing to open more restaurants.

Go wide. Think outside the restaurant: Who would have thought about putting fast food in a supermarket or in a Home Depot? Starbucks did. Some full-service restaurants have gone into airports, like Chilis Too. Restaurants have put their products into grocery stores, Target, and Walmart. To name just a few: White Castle sliders, Olive Garden dressings, P.F. Chang's chicken dumplings, Olive Garden dressings, Krispy Kreme Bites, Cinnabon Cinnamon bread, Taco Bell taco seasoning, Cheesecake Factory frozen cheesecakes, Dunkin' coffee, and Arby's curly fries.

Happy Hour: Started somewhere around 1933 during prohibition. Today, it's used as an incentive to sell drinks during slow times.

Theme restaurants: Theme restaurants started in the 1920s with novelty buildings to get noticed by passing cars, such as the Brown Derby and the Bulldog Café in Hollywood.

Massive changes in the Restaurant Industry Social Norms and Cultural Changes

Smoking to non-smoking areas, to completely non-smoking: Once upon a time, there was smoking in restaurants. Lots of smoking in restaurants. Then, the US Surgeon General came out with a report that cigarette smoking might be harmful to your health. Anti-smoking groups and peer pressure made some restaurants start to have non-smoking areas. Most of these early days designated non-smoking areas were right next to smoking areas, making the non-smoking areas a joke. Each year the percentage of tables designated as non-smoking increased until it reached 100%. At first, restaurant chains and owners complained that nonsmokers hurt their business because they usually drank less and spent less money.

Dram Shop Law: This shifted responsibility for intoxicated customers from the individual to the restaurant or bar causing restaurants and bars to greatly increase training of bartenders and servers to recognize intoxicated customers and critically examine using 2 for 1's and discounts.

COVID-19 pandemic: See chapter Bad Stuff

Minimum drinking age: The federal drinking age was raised to 21 in 1984. Before that, the minimum drinking age was left up to each state, which ranged from 16 to 21.

Healthy eating/Going organic/Farm to table/Local produce: Caused huge changes in restaurant menus.

Social media marketing and reviews: Many, many reports find that people are influenced by online reviews and comments. Today, most restaurants use social media as their primary form of advertising.

Immigration: A report by The Chicago Council on Global Affairs stated that while the US is made up of 13.7% of immigrants, immigrants make up 22 percent of food service employees and 37% of small restaurant owners.

Frozen foods: allowed restaurants to be more affordable and offer more varied menus throughout the entire year.

Women in the workplace: After WWII, women entered int the workplace in significant numbers, causing huge increases in restaurant sales.

Red meat scare – Red meat is one of the most controversial foods in nutrition. In the 1970s, a few scientists began linking red meat to cancer causing some chains, which emphasized red meat almost exclusively, like Victoria Station, to close.

Unions: In 1891, The Hotel and Restaurant Employees International Alliance was founded which became Unite Here. Burgerville, a regional fast-food chain based in Vancouver, Washington, with around 40 locations, became the first fast-food union in the US in 2021. Starbucks and Chipotle are feeling pressure to unionize.

Deeper Dive
Ghost Kitchens, Dark Kitchens

These are purpose-built to be only take-out kitchens. Kitchens are focused on take out, they don't require great locations like their brick-and-mortar brothers and sisters to attract customers and can be located in lower rent real estate or be centrally located in city centers for fast delivery to a large number of customers. Because kitchens are built for takeout only, they can serve different brands out of one kitchen because of their single delivery-only design. Yet more advantages that these kitchens have over brick-and-mortar restaurants is they require much less money to launch because they do not require the usual permitting, build-out, and staff of traditional restaurants.

Virtual Kitchens, Virtual Brands: a take-out only "restaurant" that doesn't really exist as a separate entity, but all its menu items are made inside another brick-and-mortar restaurant. Examples are Chili's 'It's Just Wings', Denny's 'Burger Den' and 'The Melt Down'.

Thank you for reading!

www.ingramcontent.com/pod-product-compliance
Lightning Source LLC
Chambersburg PA
CBHW071957290426
44109CB00018B/2051